Communications Sector-Specific Plan

An Annex to the National Infrastructure Protection Plan

2010

Homeland Security

Preface

Establishing a strategic framework for protecting the Nation's critical communications infrastructure is crucial to ensuring national security. The National Infrastructure Protection Plan (NIPP) provides the overarching framework for integrating protective programs and activities that are underway in the various critical infrastructure and key resources (CIKR) sectors. The NIPP includes 18 Sector-Specific Plans (SSPs) that detail the application of the overall risk management framework for each specific sector. The U.S. Department of Homeland Security (DHS), National Communications System (NCS) serves as the Sector-Specific Agency for the Communications Sector. Private sector owners and operators have enjoyed a close working relationship with NCS since its inception in 1963.

NCS and its partners coordinate the development and the implementation of the Communications SSP (CSSP) to reduce risk across the Communications Sector. The CSSP is intended to ensure that the Communications Sector effectively coordinates with sector partners, other sectors, and DHS to enhance protection and resilience in an all-hazards environment. The CSSP presents a vision of how the Communications Sector will manage risk utilizing both public and private resources, how partners will implement programs and practices to achieve sector goals, and how the sector will measure the success of protective activities. The CSSP is the result of close collaboration among NCS, the Communications Sector Coordinating Council, and the Communications Government Coordinating Council. It provides a framework through which industry and government partners can develop a coordinated protection strategy.

This 2010 release of the CSSP reflects the maturation of the partnership and the progress of the sector programs first outlined in the 2007 CSSP. Examples of sector accomplishments since the publication of the 2007 CSSP include:

- The Communications Sector completed the baseline Communications Sector National Risk Assessment (NSRA) in 2008 and is currently performing the 2010 NSRA.

- Sector partners placed a new emphasis on interdependencies, partnerships, coordination, and collaboration among all levels of government and with the private sector. An example is the establishment of the Telecom Energy Alliance, composed of both government and industry partners, to further the recommendations from the Critical Dependency on Electric Power Working Group.

- Sector partners participated in several exercises to test and implement network level protective strategies, including the National Cyber Incident Response Plan (NCIRP) Tabletop in support of the NCIRP, designed to assist sector partners to detect threats and rapidly restore outages caused by those with malicious intent (e.g., cyber attacks) and by natural disaster.

- The National Cybersecurity and Communications Integration Center (NCCIC), was launched in October 2009. The facility unites Communications Sector coordination of the National Coordinating Center and the cyber protection efforts of the United States Computer Emergency Readiness Team. Industry partners are currently testing industry-to-industry information-sharing to provide policy recommendations to the President and enhance NCCIC operations.

Each year, the Communications Sector CIKR Protection Annual Report will provide updates on the sector's efforts to identify, prioritize, and coordinate the protection of its critical infrastructure. The Sector Annual Report provides the current priorities of the sector as well as the progress made during the past year in following the plans and strategies set out in the CSSP.

Gregory Schaffer

Assistant Secretary for
Cybersecurity and Communications
U.S. Department of
Homeland Security

Todd M. Keil

Assistant Secretary for
Infrastructure Protection
U.S. Department of
Homeland Security

Robert Mayer

Chair
Communications Sector
Coordinating Council

Table of Contents

List of Figures

List of Tables

Executive Summary

Communications are an integral part of the Nation's health and safety, economy, and public confidence.

The U.S. Department of Homeland Security (DHS) released the National Infrastructure Protection Plan (NIPP) in 2006 to serve as a comprehensive risk management framework and address the preexisting threat environment of natural disasters, cyber attacks, and terrorism. The NIPP has since been updated and further defines critical infrastructure protection roles and responsibilities for all levels of government and private industry. DHS recognizes that a successful risk assessment framework requires cooperation and coordination among Federal departments and agencies; State, local, and tribal governments; private sector owners and operators; and international partners.

To implement the NIPP, Sector-Specific Agencies (SSAs) for each of the 18 critical infrastructure and key resources (CIKR) sectors are partnering with State, local, and tribal governments, and industry to create and implement Sector-Specific Plans (SSPs). The DHS National Communications System (NCS) serves as the SSA for the Communications Sector.

NCS and its partners coordinate the development of the Communications SSP (CSSP) to reduce risk across the Communications Sector. The CSSP is intended to ensure that the Communications Sector effectively coordinates with sector partners, other sectors, and DHS to enhance protection and resilience in an all-hazards environment. The CSSP presents a vision of how the Communications Sector will manage risk utilizing both public and private resources, how partners will implement programs and practices to achieve sector goals, and how the sector will measure the success of protective activities.

The CSSP is the result of close collaboration among NCS, the Communications Sector Coordinating Council, and the Communications Government Coordinating Council. It provides a framework through which industry and government partners can develop a coordinated protection strategy.

The Federal Government has a responsibility to develop and execute a national plan that protects the overall security of the Nation. For government partners, the processes outlined in this plan support their missions to execute command, control, and coordination; to provide national, economic, and homeland security; and to ensure public health and safety.

For private sector partners, critical infrastructure protection is critical to secure employees, assets, business continuity, and services provided to customers. Private sector companies implement protection efforts aimed at limiting the risk to the business and maintaining operational capabilities. Business leaders have a broad-level responsibility to direct these efforts and ensure effective implementation.

This plan takes into consideration the value of resilience; the growth of mobile technology; cyber threats; and continuity of service requirements for mission critical assets, systems, and networks. It also considers the need to better engage State, local, tribal, and international partners.

Background

The Nation's communications infrastructure is a complex system of systems that incorporates multiple technologies and services with diverse ownership. The infrastructure includes wireline, wireless, satellite, cable, and broadcasting capabilities, and includes the transport networks that support the Internet and other key information systems. The communications companies that own, operate, and supply the Nation's communications infrastructure have historically factored natural disasters and accidental disruptions into network resilience architecture, business continuity plans, and disaster recovery strategies. The interconnected and interdependent nature of these service provider networks has fostered crucial information-sharing and cooperative response and recovery relationships for decades. Even in today's highly competitive business environment, the community has a long standing tradition of cooperation and trust because problems with one service provider's network nearly always impact networks owned and operated by other network providers.

Most Communications Sector infrastructure are owned by the private sector; therefore, establishing a single strategic framework for protecting the Nation's critical communications infrastructure is crucial to ensuring national security. Private sector owners and operators have enjoyed a close working relationship with NCS since its inception in 1963. This relationship was further enhanced by the establishment of the National Coordinating Center (NCC) in 1984. NCC serves as a joint industry-government operations center with a clear mission of advancing information sharing and coordination. Under the aegis of NCC, many member companies participated in the design and execution of the Local Exchange Carrier Mutual Aid Agreement. This agreement was subsequently adopted in Canada and used for cross border mutual aid.

The NIPP established a common risk management framework for use by all 18 individual CIKR sectors. This framework establishes goals, assesses risks, and defines priority programs to enhance critical infrastructure protection. Figure S-1 illustrates the framework that provides the foundation for the CSSP.

Figure ES-1: NIPP Risk Management Framework

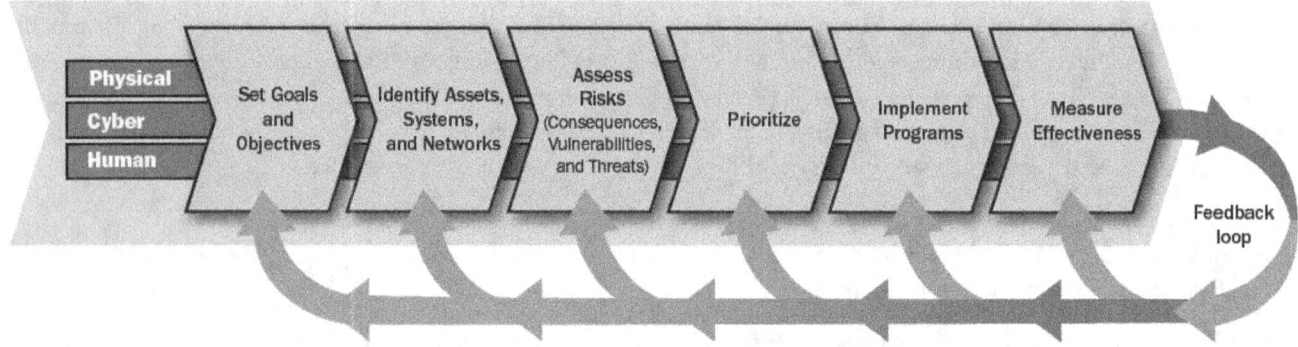

Continuous Improvement to enhance protection of CIKR

CSSP partners considered existing programs and best practices when identifying the sector's goals for securing physical, cyber, and human elements. The goals identified in the plan focus on protecting the overall health of the national communications backbone; response and recovery during and after an attack or disaster; information sharing, awareness, and education in the context of current and potential future threats; and cross-sector coordination to address critical interdependencies. The Communications Sector goals are illustrated in figure S-2.

Going Forward

The Communications Sector's infrastructure protection strategy is to ensure that the Nation's communications systems and networks are secure, resilient, and rapidly restored after an incident. The approach outlined in the CSSP includes the following:

- Utilize industry and government partnerships to protect the communications infrastructure by leveraging corporate capabilities and government programs;

- Adopt an architectural approach to infrastructure identification and risk assessment processes;

- Coordinate, plan, and provide awareness to and with other CIKR sectors on communications infrastructure dependencies and solutions for mitigating risk; and

- Work closely with DHS to improve the protection of the Communications Sector through better analysis and the improvement of CIKR.

The aim of the CSSP is to present a vision of how the Communications Sector will manage risk across the sector by utilizing both public and private resources, implementing programs and practices to achieve its goals, and measuring the effectiveness of protective activities.

Figure ES-2: Communications Sector Goals

Goal 1: Protect and enhance the overall physical and logical health of communications.

Goal 2: Rapidly reconstitute critical communications services in the event of disruption and mitigate cascading effects.

Goal 3: Improve the sector's national security and emergency preparedness (NS/EP) posture with Federal, State, local, tribal, international, and private sector entities to reduce risk.

The CSSP focuses the Communications Sector's risk management process on identifying and protecting nationally critical architecture elements; ensuring overall network reliability; maintaining "always-on" services for critical customers; and quickly restoring critical communications functions and services following a disruption.

The framework's risk assessment process analyzes threats and vulnerabilities to better understand the associated risks to critical communications infrastructure. It addresses the following:

- Significant internal measures are taken by private sector owners and operators to ensure the reliability of their services by infusing business continuity and contingency planning principles into standard business practices;

- Government and private sector programs and partnerships that support current and future protection of mission-critical and communications services are required; and

- National communications architecture and security practices are assessed to yield a comprehensive picture of risk.

The development and implementation of the CSSP encourages public and private sector partners to enhance the Nation's communications infrastructure protection framework. Sector partners will need to prioritize the actions set forth within this plan and coordinate their implementation accordingly.

Introduction

Virtually every element of modern life is now dependent on the digital infrastructure. As a result, our Nation's economic and national security relies on the security of the assets and operations of critical communications infrastructure. Past terrorist attacks and catastrophic natural disasters emphasized the need to focus our national attention on protecting the Nation's critical infrastructure and making them more resilient. Moving forward, it is essential that public and private sectors adopt a coordinated approach toward achieving joint goals for our communications infrastructure.

Over the past year, cyber exploitation activities have grown more sophisticated, targeted, and serious. The information infrastructure, including the Internet, communications networks, computer systems, and embedded processors and controllers in critical industries, is increasingly being targeted for exploitation and potentially for disruption or destruction by a growing array of unknown actors in unknown locations. Vulnerabilities will continue to multiply as public sector, private sector, and personal activities continue to move toward networked operations; as digital systems add more capabilities; and as wireless systems become ubiquitous. The public sector—Federal, State, and local governments—and the private sector share the responsibility for securing the Nation's critical communications infrastructure. Sector partners benefit from complementary skill sets, expertise, and individual resources in order to meet their shared responsibility for addressing all-hazard threats.

Communications Sector Vision and Goals

Vision Statement for the Communications Sector

The United States has a critical reliance on assured communications. The Communications Sector strives to ensure that the Nation's communications networks and systems are secure, resilient, and rapidly restored in the event of disruption.

Goals for the Communications Sector

Goal 1: Protect and enhance the overall physical and logical health of communications.

Goal 2: Rapidly reconstitute critical communications services in the event of disruption and mitigate cascading effects.

Goal 3: Improve the sector's national security and emergency preparedness (NS/EP) posture with Federal, State, local, tribal, international, and private sector entities to reduce risk.

Background

The individuals and organizations that routinely contribute to the planning and execution of initiatives to keep the Nation's communications networks resilient enough to withstand natural and manmade disasters, as well as those responsible for rapidly restoring those networks after a major disaster occurs, have partnered to create this Sector-Specific Plan (SSP). As a component of the National Infrastructure Protection Plan (NIPP), this 2010 rewrite of the Communications SSP (CSSP) acknowledges the interdependencies between the Communications Sector and other sectors within a common public-private framework defined by the Critical Infrastructure Partnership Advisory Council (CIPAC). CIPAC membership consists of private sector critical infrastructure and key resources (CIKR) owners and operators; Federal, State, local, and tribal representatives; and representative or equivalent associations.

The NIPP Framework

Compelling Events

Hurricane Katrina wreaked havoc on a three-State telecommunications infrastructure, leaving three million users without a dial tone and taking thirty-eight 911 emergency services centers and 1,000 cell phone towers out of operation. Hurricane Katrina was the most widespread natural disaster to hit the United States.

The September 11th attacks severely disrupted communications networks; a major telecommunications hub was severely damaged in the collapse of the World Trade Center buildings, affecting more than four million data circuits.

The Homeland Security Act of 2002 and subsequent Presidential strategies[1] provided the authority and direction for CIKR sectors to collaborate on ways to further protect critical infrastructure. Homeland Security Presidential Directive 7 (HSPD-7), Critical Infrastructure Identification, Prioritization, and Protection, issued by the President on December 17, 2003, provided the direction for implementation of the strategic vision.

As directed in HSPD-7, the U.S. Department of Homeland Security (DHS) led the development of the NIPP. The NIPP provides the unifying structure for the integration of a wide range of efforts for the enhanced protection and resilience of the Nation's CIKR into a single national program. The structure emphasizes risk management by promoting the use of common, repeatable, continuous improvement processes as shown in figure I-1. This encourages each sector to generate consistent, measurable objectives that are adaptive and increasingly effective over time.

To implement the NIPP, Sector-Specific Agencies (SSA) for each of the 18 CIKR sectors partner with State, local, and tribal governments, along with industry, to create and implement SSPs. The DHS National Communications System (NCS) serves as the SSA for the Communications Sector.

---

[1] The National Strategy for the Physical Protection of Critical Infrastructures and Key Assets (February 2003) and The National Strategy to Secure Cyberspace (February 2003).

Figure I-1: NIPP Risk Management Framework

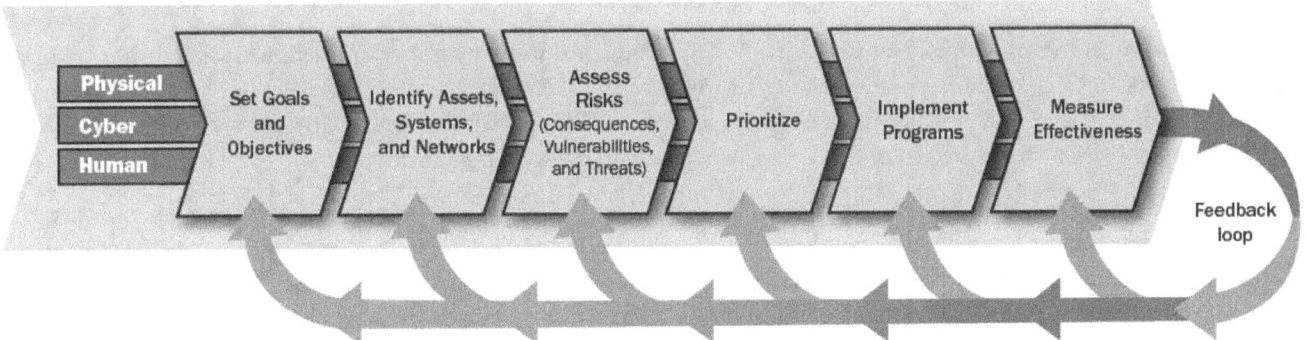

Continuous improvement to enhance protection of CIKR

The CSSP utilizes each step of the NIPP risk management framework to help identify, develop, and implement priority programs and initiatives.

Sector Coordinating Council Partnership

This CSSP results from a close collaboration among NCS, the Communications Sector Coordinating Council (CSCC), and the Communications Government Coordinating Council (CGCC). This sector partnership construct is not a recent development and has roots that go back many decades, beginning with the formation of NCS following the 1962 Cuban Missile Crisis. Over the years, the relationship has been strengthened through a focus on specific operations, planning, and strategic activities. Many of the entities that contribute to the evolving public-private partnership framework, as well as the initiatives that flow from these venues, are described in this plan.

Underlying the partnership is a broad stakeholder recognition that industry and government cannot engage effectively in national security and emergency preparedness (NS/EP) functions without the full participation and support of their respective partners. Government stakeholders understand the implications of having the vast majority of the communications infrastructure in the hands of the private sector and the need for industry to ensure that it constantly invests in the reliability and resilience of its networks. Similarly, industry partners recognize that their ability to obtain actionable threat information and to respond to disruptive events often requires a wide variety of support activities from Federal, State, and local entities. With each event, new relationships have been forged and processes have evolved to address restoration of services more efficiently. As we now respond to evolving cyber threats that exist within a complex information, communications, and technology ecosystem, the partnership construct is more relevant than ever. The emerging cyber threat environment can be addressed only in a "high-trust" environment where diverse sets of industry and government participants engage to prevent, detect, respond to, and mitigate incidents.

With each event and initiative, we expand our understanding of the complementary nature of our work and our respective capabilities. In this 2010 SSP, we take note of the considerable resources that industry and government partners will continue to commit to a broad range of objectives and specific work initiatives.

Purpose of the Communications Sector-Specific Plan

This plan is intended to enhance the Nation's communications infrastructure protection framework through collaboration of public and private sector partners. For government partners, the processes outlined in this plan support their missions to execute, command, control, and coordination; to provide national, economic, and homeland security; and to ensure public health and safety. For private sector partners, enhanced security and critical infrastructure protection are crucial for safeguarding physical, cyber, and human assets, systems, and networks; ensuring continuity of business operations; and enhancing shareholder value.

The CSSP also provides an opportunity for cross-sector collaboration on a scale that has not previously existed. Such collaboration brings value during incident response when working with other CIKR sectors becomes crucial to response and recovery efforts. This document provides a thorough set of goals and measurable objectives that will lead the sector partners closer to realizing a shared vision for ensured communications under a wide range of circumstances.

The CSSP is not an implementation plan. The CGCC and the CSCC will collaboratively develop an implementation plan that outlines activities designed to reduce risk across the Communications Sector. The CGCC/CSCC Implementation Plan will provide significant details about these activities, including their purpose, scope, budget, relevant stakeholders/participants, implementation strategy, and implementation time frame in which to initiate and complete the activities.

Scope of the Communications Sector-Specific Plan

The CSSP reflects the scope of the Communications Sector's risk management process as outlined by the NIPP. This plan outlines the infrastructure protection activities—physical, cyber, and human—through which the Communications Sector industry and government partners will individually and cooperatively mitigate risks to critical national communications infrastructure assets and services.

Organization of the Communications Sector-Specific Plan

This CSSP helps provide a common understanding of the national strategy for critical infrastructure protection in the Communications Sector. The document is organized into eight chapters. The first six chapters outline the risk management process—from setting goals to measuring progress—and match the steps in the NIPP risk management framework. The content of each chapter and its relationship to the other chapters are illustrated in figure I-2. The seventh chapter addresses research and development (R&D) and the final chapter discusses SSA responsibilities and management of the risk management and infrastructure protection process.

Figure I-2:   2010 CSSP Organizational Model

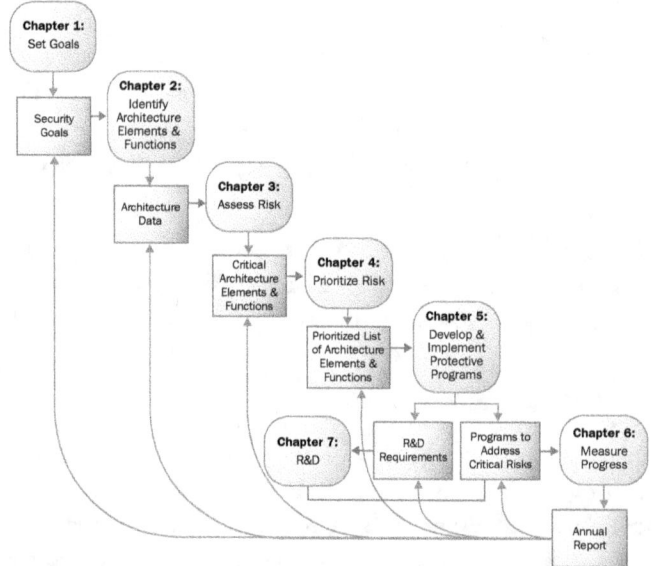

1. Establish Sector Goals and Objectives

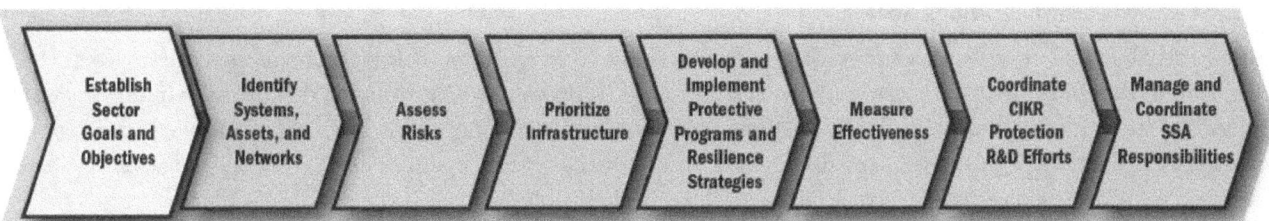

This chapter characterizes the Communications Sector, including an overview of private sector owners and operators, councils, and associations; primary Federal, State, local, tribal, and international partners; and a review of governing authorities.

1.1 Sector Profile

Over the past few decades, the sector has evolved from predominantly closed wireline telecommunications, focused on providing equipment and voice capabilities, into diverse, open, highly competitive, interconnected services with wireless, satellite, cable, and broadcast companies providing many of those same capabilities. Although market competition and standardization have helped lower prices and spurred the development of new services, these developments also have presented new challenges for those working to protect critical communications assets for NS/EP purposes.

Two key policy events helped shape the modern-day communications industry. The first event was the 1984 court-ordered breakup of AT&T, which controlled the majority of the local and long-distance markets. The second event was the passage of the Telecommunications Act of 1996, which, as the Telecommunications Act conference report states, aimed "to provide for a pro-competitive, de-regulatory national policy framework designed to accelerate rapidly private sector deployment of advanced telecommunications and information technologies and services to all Americans by opening all telecommunications markets to competition." As a result, instead of one company controlling and protecting the entire communications network, hundreds of wireline and wireless companies, including cellular and satellite, provide communications services today.

The industry continued to expand in concert with the economic boom of the late 1990s, which spurred a network-building binge within the Communications Sector. Large investments were made in new fiber facilities, helping to modernize the communications infrastructure and deliver advanced Internet services to home and business users. As the Nation began to experience an economic downturn in 2000, the communications industry saw an oversupply of capacity and a drop in prices. Capital spending declined, jobs were cut, and seasoned communications industry players and new competitors filed for bankruptcy.

In addition to these sweeping regulatory and economic changes, technological convergence has also had a profound impact on the communications industry. Whereas the public network had consisted primarily of the narrowband, mature Public Switched

Telephone Network (PSTN), it is now rapidly evolving toward wideband, packet-based next-generation networks (NGNs). In addition to the complexity associated with convergence, the Nation's communications system is characterized by a diversity of technology and intra-sector dependencies.

In the American Recovery and Reinvestment Act of 2009, Congress charged the Federal Communications Commission (FCC) with creating a national broadband plan. Congress recognized that the emergence of these new broadband networks could provide significant benefits to a wide variety of stakeholders and specifically asked the FCC to address, among other matters, the use of broadband to advance public safety and homeland security. The FCC is currently involved in a significant effort to explore how broadband technologies, tools, and innovations might aid in such areas as next-generation 911 emergency services, emergency warning systems, priority services, and cybersecurity. NS/EP recommendations are expected to be included in the FCC's 2010 National Broadband Plan and are certain to have a direct impact on many initiatives affecting the Communications Sector.

Evolution of the Communications Sector

Customer demands and business imperatives are bringing about the convergence of traditional circuit switched networks interoperating with broadband and packet-based Internet Protocol (IP) networks. The evolution of wireless, wireline, and cable networks is driving toward next-generation global communications networks. Many networks and providers have developed the capability to carry voice, video, text, and data transparently to many types of end-user devices. Mobile phones able to access an array of Web-based services are only one example of this enhanced ability.

The scale, scope, and character of network convergence are fundamentally changing the way all communications are planned for, prioritized, and ultimately delivered. Packet-switched environments place greater control capabilities at the network "edge" and rely heavily on intelligent devices to execute key functions. Advanced network management capabilities provide additional functionality, reliability, and cybersecurity.

Consequently, the transition to the NGN presents challenges for ensuring the security and availability of NS/EP communications. In this new converged environment, NS/EP communications and critical business communications are subject to an increased number of cyber threats based on inherent vulnerabilities and interdependencies that are known or are expected to exist in the converged networks.

Some vulnerabilities that existed in legacy networks present more of a challenge to the NGN. For example, the sheer number of interconnections that characterize the NGN can be exploited by cyber threats to provide rapid and far-reaching propagation of malicious payloads and other forms of cyber attacks. These and other vulnerabilities create complex risk scenarios for NS/EP communications. An additional challenge is the global nature of the converged networks and, thus, methods for managing incidents of national significance are even more critical and may require international cooperation.

Additionally, the Communications Sector is well aware of the scope and potential severity of cybersecurity threats facing CIKR. The industry has invested heavily in incident detection, prevention, and mitigation capabilities. The sector is able to gather threat information by investing capital in its networks that allows Internet activity monitoring, anomaly detection, distributed denial of service attack detection, botnet detection, malware analysis, and proprietary research into each area.

Interoperability

The DHS Office of Emergency Communications (OEC), established under Title XVIII of the Homeland Security Act of 2002 (2006), supports and promotes the ability of emergency responders to continue to communicate in the event of natural disasters, acts of terrorism, or other manmade disasters, and works to ensure, accelerate, and attain interoperable and operable emergency communications nationwide. OEC oversees the Emergency Communications Preparedness Center (ECPC); the OEC Interoperable Communications Technical Assistance Program (ICTAP); and the SAFECOM program, excluding research, development, testing, and evaluation (RDT&E), and standards elements. OEC works with public safety and emergency response agencies across all levels of government to ensure that Federal, State, local, tribal, and territorial stakeholders have a mechanism for sharing information and providing valuable input to shape national policy, as well as OEC's programmatic activities; facilitate demonstration projects of emergency communications solutions; coordinate interoperable emergency communications grant guidance across all Federal programs; and provide direct technical assistance support to Federal, State, local, and tribal agencies through the development and delivery of training, tools, and on-site support.

Alerting

Executive Order (E.O.) 13407 mandated the Integrated Public Alert and Warning System (IPAWS) in 2006. IPAWS is the Nation's next-generation public alert and warning capability. The Federal Emergency Management Agency (FEMA) and the IPAWS Program Management Office are working with public and private entities to integrate warning systems that will allow the President and authorized officials to address and warn the general public and emergency operations centers via multiple communications pathways. During State and local emergencies, IPAWS gives State and local government and emergency management officials the capability to alert and warn their local populations.

Mobility

As mobility has become ubiquitous, public and private customers are coming to expect a broader array of services that facilitate "anytime, anywhere" communications. The industry continues to invest heavily to expand coverage and meet geometric increases in capacity to satisfy demand. These upgrades include replacing or updating equipment located in thousands of switching centers and hundreds of thousands of cellular sites every three to five years to support next-generation protocols.

Disaster victims and NS/EP customers place an especially high value on communications tools that are light, compact, and portable. In many cases, these escalating expectations must be checked because mobile communications rely on finite radio links. During disasters, people are on the move, and they will create spikes in demand that can overwhelm mobile network capacity. Challenging radio frequency environments may limit coverage or capacity. Damage to the underlying landline or power infrastructure may curtail the availability of mobile services.

The Communications Sector will continue to work closely with various Federal agencies to educate users on the limitations of these technologies and to encourage users of critical applications to select a robust set of communications tools. The sector also works hand-in-hand with regulatory bodies to update and deploy best practices to bolster network reliability.

The Internet

The Communications Sector is responsible for ensuring the availability of a viable NS/EP communications infrastructure and recognizes that the Internet is a key resource, which is composed of assets within both the Information Technology (IT) Sector and the Communications Sector. Originally focused on traditional telephone security services, the Communications Sector has taken on a larger role in Internet security-related issues because of the convergence of the infrastructure that serves traditional telephone voice traffic and the Internet infrastructure that serves data traffic.

More specifically, the sector implements network-based cybersecurity as an important added layer of protection that complements edge-based (firewall/antivirus software) and personnel-oriented (policies/procedures) steps. Network service operators possess situational awareness capabilities that can, depending on the nature of the cyber incident and threat vectors, often detect issues early and can provide remedial steps that permit ongoing operations of customer applications.

Managed network security services can provide customers with the highest level of security protection. Network management capabilities are essential for protecting the Nation's infrastructure against cyber attacks. However, there are legal barriers that frequently prevent the Communications Sector from being able to use this intelligence to protect other networks. For example, liability issues often inhibit the use of available information gathered from attack observations.

Reach and Impact

Other critical infrastructure are highly dependent on communications for basic operations. The services offered or performed by the Communications Sector are critical components of the business and government processes that are fundamental to our way of life; these services include electricity, banking and finance, emergency services, and government continuity of operations (COOP).

Sector Characterization

Driven by 21st century technology transformation and convergence, the Communications Sector and the IT Sector are becoming more closely aligned over time. The Communications Sector includes not only physical properties such as wireline, wireless, satellite, cable, and broadcasting, but also services such as Internet content and routing, information services, and cable television (CATV) networks. In addition, publicly and privately owned cyber/logical assets are inextricably linked with these physical communications structures. Brief descriptions of each component follow. Detailed descriptions of each component are provided in appendix D.

- **Wireline:** The wireline component consists primarily of the PSTN and includes cable networks and enterprise networks. Traditionally, it has been divided between interexchange carriers (IXCs) and local exchange carriers (LECs), but following passage of the Telecommunications Act of 1996, new competitive local exchange carriers (CLECs) entered the local, long distance, and data services markets, as did some traditional CATV providers. Today, many larger carriers operate in various areas of the Nation in all of the capacities listed above. Wireline networks also are being redefined by NGNs, which are high-speed, converged circuit-switched and packet switched networks capable of transporting and routing a multitude of services, including voice, data, video, and other multimedia, across various platforms. The wireline component also includes the Internet infrastructure and submarine cable infrastructure.

- **Wireless:** The wireless component consists primarily of cellular telephone, paging, personal communications services, high-frequency radio, unlicensed wireless, and other commercial and private radio services, including numerous law enforcement, public safety, and land mobile radio systems.

- **Satellite:** Satellite communications systems deliver data, voice, and video services. Networks may be private and independent of the terrestrial infrastructure or may share common facilities (e.g., a teleport) and may be combined with terrestrial services to deliver information to the intended recipient(s). Satellite services exist in several forms: fixed, transportable, on the move, and handheld. The technology can deliver two-way point-to-point or mesh converged access and/or backbone services (voice, data, and video), as well as multicast (video and/or data for distribution of content to large audiences).

- **Cable:** Cable communications systems are wireline networks that offer analog and digital video programming services, digital telephone service, and high-speed Internet access service. Cable systems use a mixture of fiber and coaxial cable that provide two-way signal paths to the customer. This hybrid fiber coaxial (HFC) architecture effectively segments the cable system into a number of parallel distribution networks. The HFC architecture is typically based on a three-level topology, which includes a headend, one or more distribution hub(s), and multiple fiber nodes.

- **Broadcasting:** Broadcasting systems consist of free, over-the-air radio and television stations that offer analog and digital audio and video programming services and data services. Broadcasting has been the principal means of providing emergency alert services to the public for six decades. Broadcasting systems operate in three frequency bands: medium frequency (MF), used for AM radio; very high frequency (VHF), used for FM radio and television; and ultra-high frequency (UHF), also used for television. The recent transition to digital television (DTV) and the ongoing transition to digital radio both provide broadcast stations with enhanced capabilities, including the ability to multicast multiple programs on a single channel.

While the private sector owns the vast majority of critical infrastructure, government and public safety agencies own and operate communications systems that support their critical missions, including defense, law enforcement, and public safety. The U.S. Department of Defense (DoD), for example, owns and operates communications systems in at least four of its components. Public safety agencies are heavily vested in wireless communications (e.g., land mobile radio) for disaster response.

Authorities

Key authorities for the Communications Sector address the availability, resilience, and security of the communications infrastructure and provide guidance on sector coordination and specific programs. The Federal Government does not require the private sector members of the Communications Sector to conduct vulnerability assessments or implement protective measures. The private sector conducts such activities internally to improve processes and provide better service quality. For a more detailed listing of sector authorities, refer to appendix C.

Dependencies and Interdependencies

As mentioned above, the Communications Sector is integrally linked with the IT Sector, which is composed of entities—often owners and operators and their respective associations—who produce and provide hardware, software, and IT systems and services, including development, integration, operations, communications, and security. These IT Sector products are employed across other critical infrastructure and government networks. The IT and Communications Sectors share many collocation facilities for switching and routing functions. The IT Sector depends on carrier cable networks and satellite communications for the delivery and distribution of critical functions.

To fully understand and determine an acceptable level of risk, all sectors must understand their dependence on and interdependence with communications infrastructure. The sector works with industry and all levels of government to identify cross-sector critical dependencies by leveraging existing industry and government cross-sector groups, task forces, and other mechanisms. In the past two years, NCS has performed communications infrastructure analyses in support of its Federal mission essential functions (MEFs). These analyses examined NCS MEF dependence on communications in four high consequence scenarios: (1) high altitude nuclear burst, (2) ground-based nuclear burst, (3) solar superstorm, and (4) cyber attack.

The Communications Sector, in collaboration with the Energy Sector, completed a cross-sector analysis of the Communications Sector's dependence on commercially available power sources. Communications Dependency on Electric Power (hereinafter referred to as the CDEP report), published in February 2009, addressed the potential for long-term outages and the sector's ability to recover from them. The CDEP report also examined key cross-sector organizations, agreements, policies, and guidelines.

National Coordinating Center (NCC) for Communications members continue to work with existing sector coordination groups (e.g., Information Sharing and Analysis Centers (ISACs) and Sector Coordinating Councils (SCCs)) on procedures for cross-sector incident management (e.g., the National Cybersecurity and Communications Integration Center (NCCIC)) and the sharing of situational awareness information during incidents. NCS continues to coordinate with other SSAs to conduct diversity assessments for high-risk critical infrastructure and NS/EP user facilities.

To further develop the capabilities required to address these cross-sector dependencies, industry and government will continue to plan and participate in emergency response training and exercises that address a spectrum of threats across sectors, testing coordination mechanisms, situational awareness, and incident management.

Challenges

As the Communications Sector evolves, shared infrastructure could become more vulnerable to disruptions in service due to threats presented by terrorist and other malicious attacks, by natural disasters, and by human failure to adhere to best practices intended to ensure security. During emergencies, the transmission of critical information is often interrupted because of limitations in the amount of radio frequency spectrum over which a wireless service provider can send information, combined with spikes in attempts to access the Internet. The Communications Sector faces a major challenge in managing network resources and educating all users, including emergency responders, regarding the need for diverse access methods to the Internet to ensure that emergency communications are operable. The inability of emergency responders to get information where it is needed is a major concern. Communications Sector representatives from both industry and government are working together to resolve such issues.

Relationships in the Communications Sector span a multitude of private sector, government, and international organizations. In the Communications Sector, partnerships are the foundation for all protective programs. NCS manages various communications partnerships that aim to improve all hazards response, promotes physical and cybersecurity situational awareness and the exchange of information through the NCC and the Network Security Information Exchanges (NSIE), participates in the Cross-Sector Cyber Security Working Group (CSCSWG), and closely collaborates with the National Security Telecommunications Advisory Committee (NSTAC) and the Committee of Principals. Furthermore, the effective implementation of the CSSP is due to the Communications Sector partners' excellent and longstanding partnership.

NCS Leadership

As the Communications SSA, NCS will continue to work with the 24 Federal departments and agencies represented on its Committee of Principals, as well as with private industry, to advance Communications Sector goals. It works closely with the National Cyber Security Division (NCSD), DHS Office of Infrastructure Protection, FEMA, OEC, and other departments and agencies to build effective critical infrastructure protection and emergency response partnerships to address interdependencies.

1.2 CIKR Partners

The Communications Sector has a long history of cooperation within its membership and with the Federal Government with respect to NS/EP communications. This history distinguishes the Communications Sector from most other critical sectors identified in the NIPP. The sector personifies cooperation and trusted relationships that have resulted in the delivery of critical services when emergencies and disasters occur. This strong bond exists largely because of three organizations that have been created in response to earlier threats to the Nation's critical infrastructure. Collectively, these organizations, in concert with NCS, which serves as the SSA for the Communications Sector, provide the *policy, planning, and operations* framework necessary to address the Nation's communications priorities.

NSTAC was created in 1982 by E.O. 12382. It provides a highly successful example of how industry helps inform government decisions about NS/EP communications. NSTAC comprises up to 30 chief executives from major telecommunications companies, network service providers, IT firms, financial firms, and aerospace companies. Through a deliberative process, NSTAC provides the President with recommendations intended to ensure vital telecommunications links during any event or crisis, and to help the Federal Government maintain a reliable, secure, and resilient national communications posture. Key areas of NSTAC focus include strengthening national security, enhancing cybersecurity, maintaining the global communications infrastructure, ensuring communications for disaster response, and addressing critical infrastructure interdependencies.

In 1982, Federal Government and telecommunications industry officials identified the need for a joint mechanism to coordinate the initiation and restoration of NS/EP communications services. In 1984, E.O. 12472 created the NCC. This industry government partnership advances collaboration on operational issues on a 24/7 basis and coordinates NS/EP responses in times of crisis. Since 2000, the NCC's Communications ISAC (C-ISAC), comprised of 51 member companies, has facilitated the exchange of information among industry and government participants regarding vulnerabilities, threats, intrusions, and anomalies affecting the telecommunications infrastructure. Weekly meetings of industry and government members are held to share threat and incident information. During emergencies, daily or more frequent meetings are held with industry and government personnel involved with the response effort.

The CSCC was chartered in 2005. It was established to help coordinate initiatives to improve the physical security and cybersecurity of sector assets; to ease the flow of information within the sector, across sectors, and with designated Federal agencies; and to address issues related to response and recovery following an incident or event. The 40 members of the CSCC broadly represent the sector and include cable, commercial and public broadcasters, information service providers, satellite, undersea cable, telecommunications utility providers, service integrators, equipment vendors, wireless and wireline owners and operators, and the members' respective trade associations. In 2006, the CSCC completed its first CSSP (published in 2007), which highlighted the processes to identify high-level, nationally critical architecture elements. In 2008, the CSCC completed its work on the National Sector Risk Assessment (NSRA) as prescribed by the NIPP. Its other activities have included the development of a Communications Pandemic Influenza Planning Guideline and Webinar for owners and operators, the advancement of access and credentialing solutions, and the implementation of emergency wireless protocols. The CSCC and IT SCC maintain close coordination on a range of policy and operational initiatives. The public-private partnership is manifested continuously through the regular engagement between the industry SCCs and the government counterpart GCCs.

Federal Partners

FEMA administers the alert and warning system for DHS in partnership with the DHS Science and Technology (S&T) Directorate, the FCC, the National Oceanic and Atmospheric Administration, the U.S. Department of Justice (DOJ), Office of Justice Programs for AMBER Alerts, the Joint Interoperability Test Command, and other Federal partners. The IPAWS Program Management Office is also engaged with the FEMA regions in order to coordinate the requirements of State, regional, and local emergency managers.

The American public is the Communications Sector's greatest stakeholder. As with any disaster situation, it is the strength and resilience of the American people that ameliorates the initial devastating impact of a disaster—regardless of its origin. FEMA and the IPAWS Program Management Office will work to ensure, through the many forums and venues available, that the needs and concerns of the public are known and integrated into the next generation of alert and warning systems. IPAWS stakeholders from the private sector include the Society of Broadcast Engineers, the National Association of Broadcasters, the Association of Public Television Stations, the International Association of Emergency Managers, the National Emergency Management Association, the Public Broadcasting Service, and the Organization for the Advancement of Structured Information Standards.

State and Local Partners

Relationships with State and local agencies in the Communications Sector focus primarily on regulatory issues with State public utility commissions (PUCs), State and local emergency operations centers, and emergency response activities with first responders and 911 emergency services centers. Since 2001, Federal entities have been coordinating homeland security initiatives by establishing information-sharing relationships within the Federal Government and with States and cities, and conducting vulnerability assessments of their communications networks.

The State, Local, Tribal, and Territorial Government Coordinating Council (SLTTGCC) serves as a forum to ensure that State, local, tribal, and territorial homeland security partners are fully integrated as active participants in national CIKR protection efforts and to provide an organizational structure to coordinate across their jurisdictions on State- and local-level CIKR protection guidance, strategies, and programs. The SLTTGCC provides input and suggestions for implementation to the NIPP, including sector protection programs and initiatives. These types of engagements foster broad public sector partner involvement to actively develop CIKR protection priorities and requirements.

The Multi-State Information Sharing and Analysis Center's (MS-ISAC) mission is to provide a common mechanism to raise the level of cybersecurity readiness and response in each State and with local governments. The MS-ISAC provides a central resource for gathering information from States on cyber threats to critical infrastructure and provides two-way sharing of information between and among the States and with local government.

The Regional Consortium Coordinating Council (RCCC) is the recognized forum for coordination among regional partnerships for the purpose of critical infrastructure protection and resilience. Cross-sector and multi-jurisdictional CIKR protection challenges provide an opportunity to manage interdependent risks at the regional level. Individually, the activities of the regional consortium enhance the physical security, cybersecurity, emergency preparedness, and overall public-private continuity and resilience of one or more States, urban areas, or municipalities. The RCCC provides a unique mechanism to integrate NIPP implementation on a regional scale and details its efforts in the RCCC Annual Report.

Communications Liaisons are NCS staff members designated to support geographic regions of the country to promote priority services communications programs to emergency response organizations and State and local leaders; coordinate with State and local government officials on emergency communications policy, training, and operations; and serve as regional emergency communications staff in the event of a disaster or security event.

The National Association for Regulatory Utility Commissioners (NARUC) functions as the Federal Government's main interface with State utility regulators. NARUC serves the public interest by improving the quality and effectiveness of public utility regulation.

The National Cyber Incident Response Plan (NCIRP) Committee's objective is to partner with volunteers from the 18 CIKR sectors, States, and Federal agencies (including those within DHS) to develop a National Cyber Incident Response Plan.

The Statewide Interoperability Coordinators (SWICs) Council comprises the communications interoperability coordinators and Statewide Communication Interoperability Plan (SCIP) points of contact from each of the 50 States and six Territories. OEC supports the SWICs in the implementation of their SCIP and equips the SWICs with tools, best practices, and policy information. Additionally, OEC engages the SWICs to gain input on OEC policies and programs. The SWICs meet in person twice a year.

The SAFECOM Executive Committee (EC) and the Emergency Response Council (ERC) comprise State, local, and tribal emergency response officials and association representatives and provides input to OEC and the Office for Interoperability and Compatibility (OIC) on emergency communications policies, programs, and initiatives. OEC engages the EC and ERC regularly, with monthly, quarterly, and biannual meetings.

The Critical Infrastructure Partnership Advisory Council (CIPAC) was established by DHS to facilitate more effective coordination of Federal infrastructure protection programs with the infrastructure protection activities of the private sector and the State, local, tribal, and territorial governments. CIPAC membership encompasses CIKR owner and operator institutions—and their designated trade or equivalent organizations—that are identified as members of existing SCCs. CIPAC also includes representatives from Federal, State, local, and tribal government entities identified as members of existing GCCs for each sector.

The Economic Security Working Group, which has both industry and government membership, meets in alternating months to share information on new domestic and international physical and cyber security issues across the industrial spectrum.

The CIKR Cross-Sector Council includes representatives from the SCC leadership of each sector through the **Partnership for Critical Infrastructure Security (PCIS)**. The mission of the CIKR Cross-Sector Council is to coordinate cross-sector initiatives that promote public and private efforts to help ensure secure, safe, and reliable critical infrastructure services. This mission encompasses physical, cyber, and human security that rely on strong infrastructure integrity and resilience.

The Federal Partnership for Interoperable Communications (FPIC) addresses Federal wireless communications interoperability by fostering intergovernmental cooperation. It is a coordinating body that focuses on technical and operational matters within the Federal wireless communications community, representing more than 40 Federal entities. FPIC has four standing committees that meet monthly to focus on interoperability, security, spectrum, and standards.

The Protected Critical Infrastructure Information (PCII) Program was established pursuant to the Critical Infrastructure Information (CII) Act of 2002. The program institutes a means for the voluntary sharing of private sector, State, and local CIKR information with the Federal Government while providing assurance that the information will be exempt from public disclosure and will be properly safeguarded.

The Homeland Infrastructure Threat Risk Analysis Center (HITRAC) conducts integrated threat analysis for all CIKR sectors, bringing together intelligence and infrastructure specialists to ensure a complete understanding of the risks to U.S. CIKR. HITRAC works in partnership with the U.S. intelligence and law enforcement communities to integrate and analyze available threat information. HITRAC also partners with the SSAs and owners and operators to ensure that their expertise on infrastructure operations is integrated into threat analysis.

State and Local Regulatory Partners

State and local agencies have jurisdiction over communications providers within their boundaries regarding individual requirements related to providing service and constructing networks. The State PUC is the primary authority for implementing these regulations. Individual communications carriers work directly with State PUCs regularly to address regulatory issues. As noted in the Authorities section, some States have requirements for communications carriers that are related to CIKR protection, such as providing critical infrastructure asset information. State regulators and other agencies typically have working relationships with the sector that far exceed their regulatory role in the sector. For example, in States with hundreds of local telephone companies, regulators are well positioned to play an important role in providing the interface between government support and utility activity on protection and preparedness.

Within the 2009 CDEP report, "situational awareness tools" were recommended as a means of assisting in resource allocation during an emergency in order to share information across sectors and States. The report states that the situational analysis tools employed in managing the response to a major disaster should be the same ones that are employed in managing the day-to-day activities and in training and exercises. The report also identifies available cross-sector situational analysis tools that facilitate information sharing, and similar situational analysis tools, which assist in resource allocation at the macro-level during an emergency. Whether preparing for long-term electric power outages or for national disasters, it is important for industry and government to agree on cross-sector situational analysis data structures and tools to help create a common operating picture and eliminate duplicative activities. The CDEP report recommended that government work closely with industry to support the creation and development of cross-sector situational analysis tools to facilitate information sharing in advance of, during, and after a disaster.[2]

NARUC presides over the Committee on Critical Infrastructure, which focuses on identifying the proper role for PUCs with respect to the security of the Nation's electric, natural gas, communications, and water infrastructure from all-hazard threats.[3] This committee acts as the primary point of contact (POC) for Federal agencies on CIKR protection issues related to States' public utilities. In addition, through the committee, NARUC-member commissions have partnered with Federal agencies and engaged in analysis, coordination, and institutional network-building programs that facilitate CIKR protection and improved emergency response. NARUC also is represented in numerous Federal and private sector partnerships, including the Communications Security, Reliability, and Interoperability Council (CSRIC); the U.S. Department of Transportation's Enhanced 911 (E-911) Working Group; the FCC's State E 911 Working Group; and the GCC for the Energy Sector.

International Partners

The Communications Sector collaborates internationally on a number of fronts regarding NS/EP and critical infrastructure protection. NCS, in cooperation with DHS and the U.S. Department of State (DOS), actively assesses the work of multilateral organizations such as the United Nations (UN), the European Union (EU), the Organization of American States (OAS), and

---

2 See chapter 5 and the appendices of the CDEP report.

3 The FCC and DHS are also members of the Ad Hoc Committee.

the Asia-Pacific Economic Cooperation (APEC). NCS also participates in the International Telecommunication Union (ITU), an organization within the UN, where governments and the private sector coordinate global communications networks, services, and standards.

Communications networks are global in scope; hence, it is important that infrastructure protection activities for the sector extend beyond U.S. borders. Industry and government are actively involved in international organizations and multilateral/bilateral relationships in order to share lessons learned, discuss best practices, and set standards.

NCS and OEC have a strong working relationship with Canada on NS/EP communications and critical infrastructure protection issues. The United States and Canada created the Civil Emergency Planning Telecommunications Advisory Group (CEPTAG) in 1988 to address shared communications concerns, as well as to facilitate cross-border cooperation and mutual assistance in the event of an emergency. NCS also enjoys a well-developed bilateral relationship with the United Kingdom, which is pursued primarily through the Joint Contact Group (JCG). The principal NCS task under the JCG is to develop government-to-government priority routing capability for emergency communications. NCS will continue to collaborate with industry and government partners to strengthen these and other key bilateral relationships.

NCS is also involved in the implementation of the Security and Prosperity Partnership of North America (SPP). The SPP was launched in 2005 as a multi-national effort to increase security and enhance prosperity in North America. NCS leads several initiatives within the SPP as part of the larger effort to develop and implement a common approach to critical infrastructure protection and plans for response to cross-border terrorist incidents and natural disasters. NCS also represents the U.S. Government within the North Atlantic Treaty Organization's (NATO) Civil Communications Planning Committee (CCPC). The CCPC works to assess existing and future civil postal and telecommunications systems, networks, and other resources relative to civil emergency planning and critical infrastructure protection in response to natural and manmade disasters. The NCS International Affairs Advisor leads the U.S. delegation to the CCPC, along with an NCC industry representative and colleagues from the U.S. Postal Service.

1.3 Sector Goals and Objectives

With the wide range of companies, technologies, and government interests that make up the Communications Sector, it is important to find common ground in establishing sector goals. The goals represent specific outcomes, conditions, end points, and performance targets for the sector, and provide a framework for the remainder of the SSP, guiding the sector's focus on resources and protective measures and giving the sector a means by which to evaluate its progress and performance.

A collaborative process for setting sector goals for the industrial and governmental components of the sector was necessary to ensure that the goals accurately reflect the protective posture and priorities of all sector partners. NCS began the process with a facilitated offsite meeting to draft a set of goals where participants included a small group of industry partners and NCS representatives.[4] This dialogue was continued during a series of meetings in which industry and government partners further refined sector goals. A broader distribution of partners had subsequent opportunities to comment on and revise the goals during numerous comment periods.

In developing the goals, participants considered many dimensions of the protective spectrum. In many cases, sector partners referenced existing programs and best practices to set the sector goals for securing physical, cyber, and human assets. Within this structure, the sector goals cover the following categories:

• Protection and resilience;

• Response and recovery;

---

[4] The first meeting was held July 28–29, 2005.

- Awareness; and

- Cross-sector coordination.

Although all of these are critical, preserving the overall health of the communications backbone[5] is the sector's first priority at the national level. The sector acknowledges that resilience and its ability to withstand disruptions is critical; however, the integrity and security of the backbone is the sector's main focus from a protection standpoint.

Figure 1-1 below outlines the Communications Sector vision, goals, and objectives. The eight chapters within this CSSP are organized around the objectives set forth within the figure below.

Figure 1-1: Communications Sector Vision, Goals, and Objectives

Vision
The United States has a critical reliance on assured communications. The Communications Sector strives to ensure that the Nation's communications networks and systems are secure, resilient, and rapidly restored in the event of disruption.

Goals
Goal 1: Protect and enhance the overall physical and logical health of communications.
Goal 2: Rapidly reconstitute critical communications services during a disruption and mitigate cascading effects.
Goal 3: Improve the sector's national security and emergency preparedness posture with Federal, State, local, tribal, international, and private sector entities to reduce risk.

Objectives							
1. Establish Sector Goals and Objectives	2. Identify Systems, Assets, and Networks	3. Assess Risks	4. Prioritize Infrastructure	5. Develop and Implement Protective Programs and Resilience Strategies	6. Measure Effectiveness	7. Coordinate CIKR Protection R&D Efforts	8. Manage and Coordinate SSA Responsibilities

1.4 Value Proposition

The full engagement of the Communications Sector—industry and government—is essential for the CSSP to achieve its goals and support the NIPP. The Communications Sector brings value to the community and its citizens through measures employed to better protect against and rapidly recover from any event, catastrophic or otherwise, that could potentially damage, disrupt, or destroy its critical assets, systems, networks, and functions. The Communications Sector leverages robust business continuity plans that combine threat and vulnerability assessments and countermeasures with sound business practices to guide the ownership and management of critical infrastructure under its control. Industry's extensive experience protecting, restoring, and reconstituting the communications infrastructure is invaluable in enabling Federal and other government partners to predict, anticipate, and understand how communications failures affect the ability to communicate during times of crisis, impact the operations of other infrastructure, and affect response and recovery efforts.

The development and implementation of the CSSP provides an opportunity for industry and government sector partners to take advantage of a common infrastructure protection framework. For government partners, the processes outlined in this plan support their missions to execute command, control, and coordination; to provide national, economic, and homeland security; and to ensure public health and safety. For private sector partners, the protection of critical infrastructure is important for the security of their employees, assets, business continuity, and services provided to customers.

---

[5] The communications backbone is inclusive of the core wireline network and Internet backbone. In this document, backbone will primarily be used to refer to the core network/Internet backbone.

The Communications Sector provides additional value to NS/EP and critical infrastructure protection efforts through the following:

- **Development of Security Best Practices.** Best practices are derived from insights from both the historic technical support experience of individual companies and proactive efforts to address communications infrastructure vulnerabilities. Through the risk management strategies outlined in the CSSP, industry and government are engaged in creating new best practices and further confirming the value of existing best practices, while simultaneously improving network reliability.

- **Timely Access to Needed Resources.** Sector partnerships provide priority communications services that ensure the communications infrastructure's ability to meet NS/EP requirements under all circumstances. The key partners and users of these priority services and programs are those responsible for minimizing loss of life and restoring order and critical services following a major disaster. These groups include Federal, State, and local government leaders and the senior leadership of the Nation's critical infrastructure and key communications and IT industries and organizations. Access to these programs helps facilitate priority status for restoration of services (e.g., power) and enhances the direction of recovery efforts.

- **Government Support for R&D Initiatives.** The CSSP helps to identify and prioritize R&D initiatives that are important to the Communications Sector. To accomplish this effort, Federal R&D initiatives are reviewed that have the potential to meet the communications challenges identified in the CSSP, a gap analysis is conducted, potential projects are mapped to the sector's identified technology gaps, and a report summarizing the initiatives is produced.

2. Identify Assets, Systems, and Networks

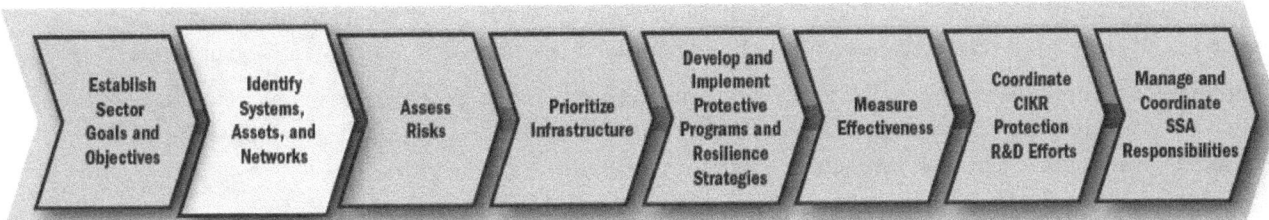

The CSSP's highest priority is to highlight the process of identifying and protecting nationally critical architecture elements, ensure the overall reliability of the networks, maintain "always on" capabilities for certain critical customers, and quickly restore essential communications services following a disruption. Nationally critical elements are assets, networks, systems, or functions that, if destroyed, disrupted, or exploited, would seriously threaten national security, result in catastrophic health effects or mass casualties, weaken the economy, or damage public morale and confidence. This chapter describes the processes used in the Communications Sector for identifying high-level architecture infrastructure as part of the overall risk management effort. These include defining information parameters and identifying, collecting, verifying, updating, and protecting infrastructure information.

As a result of the overall resilience and the dynamic nature of communications technology, the Communications Sector adopted a high-level architectural approach to concentrate on nationally critical elements. Physical communications assets are deemed critical based on the role that the asset plays in the continued operation of the core network or based on that asset being essential to a critical service or mission of another critical infrastructure sector. Logical elements also may be designated as critical, depending on the function that they provide to end users in an affected area and the maximum allowable outage before impacting user missions. The overall Communications Sector risk management methodology is neither purely asset-based nor purely systems-based, but instead is a hybrid of both approaches.

The identification of sector high-level architecture elements is an important theme of the CSSP. For example, one of the sector's goals is to have a secure and resilient national communications core network, because its main function is to carry national and international traffic between primary network nodes. Analysis of the network core focuses on identifying the primary architecture elements instead of all of the specific physical and/or logical assets in the access or other distribution networks and their individual owners. The Communications Sector collaborates with the IT Sector on the identification of Internet architecture elements. The sector compiles and uses Internet architecture information in specific components of the national risk assessment process.

The Communications Sector's high-level architectural approach factors in the individual responsibilities for addressing risk, which fall into three categories: owner and operator risk; owner, operator, and customer risk; and customer risk.

- **Owner and Operator Risk:** Owners and operators are responsible for mitigating the risk to the communications core network and signaling and control systems that are related to the operations of the communications infrastructure. They also share the responsibility for mitigating risk to assets and systems shared by multiple operators.

- **Owner, Operator, and Customer Risk:** Owners, operators, and customers share responsibility for the access portion of the network, particularly because the location and the characteristics of the customer's premises significantly influence the access arrangement. Although owners and operators accept responsibility for maintaining the access portion of the network and restoring/reconstituting it in a timely manner after an event, customers must accept the risk that the access portion of the network may be disrupted and should adopt mitigation strategies as appropriate. Large customers often negotiate service-level agreements to guarantee service availability or the quality of service as a measure to reduce risk. Customers may mitigate the access risk by, among other approaches, locating their mission-critical functions in at least two geographically diverse locations and ensuring that those locations have two independent access connections, providing for physically diverse cable entrances and physically diverse communication technologies, and procuring diverse primary and backup services.

- **Customer Risk:** Customers are responsible for accepting and mitigating risk to their own communications assets and systems. Customer enterprise infrastructure is often a limiting factor during incidents. Without proper planning, enterprise network users may not have reliable access to their internal systems.

Federal and State governments play multiple roles in mitigating the risk to the Communications Sector, including infrastructure protection planning, enabling response and recovery operations, assisting with risk assessments, participating in cross-sector assessments, and implementing national protective programs. However, Federal and State governments can fall into more than one of the risk assignment groups. For example, Federal, State, local, and tribal governments and end users of communications services are also customers and thus have responsibilities for risk assigned under "customer risk," as described above. Likewise, some departments and agencies also have responsibilities as owners and operators of specific government communications infrastructure.

The Communications Sector recognizes the importance of addressing cross-sector dependencies on communications. In terms of the responsibility for risk, other CIKR sectors are typically considered to be customers. Communications Sector industry and government partners are committed to working with other CIKR sectors to address cross-sector dependencies through customer relationships, as well as through other SSAs and sector partnerships.

2.1 Defining Information Parameters

The resilience of the assets, programs, technology, and systems that compose the communications infrastructure reduce the likelihood of a significant national-level network failure. For example, the sector achieves resilience through the technology and redundancy employed in designing networks and by encouraging customers to employ diverse primary and backup communications capabilities. Communications network owners and operators employ technology and protocols (e.g., mesh networks, synchronous optical network (SONET) rings, and routing protocols), creating effective self-healing networks and helping to mitigate risk at the design stage. Sector owners and operators focus on ensuring overall network reliability, maintaining "always on" capabilities for customers, and quickly restoring capabilities following a disruption.

The sector is characterized primarily by the architecture elements of the assets, systems, networks, and cyber infrastructure. Architecture elements in the Communications Sector include the following:

- **Assets:** Assets include equipment collocation facilities, systems shared by network operators, and equipment owned and operated by the end user or located at the end user's facility. Customers include individuals, businesses, and government.

- **Systems:** Systems are signaling and control systems that exchange information about establishing a connection and that control the management of the network. They also access, primarily, the local portion of the network, which connects end users to the core that enables users to send or receive communications. Access includes equipment and systems such as PSTN switches, asynchronous transfer mode (ATM) switches, video servers for video on demand, and IP routers for Internet service providers (ISPs).

- **Networks:** These high-capacity core network elements service nationwide, regional, and international connectivity.

- **Cyber infrastructure:** All sector assets, systems, and networks include cyber infrastructure elements. Cyber infrastructure is composed of people, process, and technological elements that enable the efficient and effective functioning of information and computer systems, as well as the generation, transmission, and delivery of data, voice, and video over fixed and mobile assets. People elements include computer emergency response teams (CERTs), watch floors, coordination centers, and international information-sharing venues like the Forum of Incident Response and Security Teams (FIRSTs) and the North American Network Operators Group (NANOG). Process elements include sector and enterprise policies, concept of operations plans, and response plans. Technological elements include routers, switches, protocols, and other specialized hardware and software.

Cyber Risk Management

Cyber risk management often parallels and is complementary to physical and human-focused risk management. In both dimensions, it includes initiatives and practices focused on people, processes, and technology. Communications networks are dynamic, especially in the cyber dimension, or the information systems and infrastructure elements of those networks. Cybersecurity measures include encryption, independent third-party security posture assessments, employee screening and recurring security awareness training, and business continuity planning. Cyber risk management should be conducted in concert with other risk management, in support of organizational and sector objectives.

Because of the borderless nature of the cyber dimension and the speed of information flow, cyber dependencies are both difficult to measure and international by default. Exploits of a vulnerability introduced halfway around the world can begin affecting critical U.S. communications components in a matter of minutes. Therefore, Communications Sector owners and operators employ robust sensors, including intrusion detection and prevention systems, network flow management technologies, supply chain risk management best practices and acquisition support, filters, and human elements with global contacts, to provide as much early warning as possible. The sector also works closely with the IT Sector, especially the Information Technology ISAC (IT-ISAC), the United States Computer Emergency Readiness Team (US-CERT), and global CERT teams.

Interdependencies are cross-border and cross-sector by nature and are unique from region to region. One of the best ways to discover and subsequently manage interdependencies is by conducting regional exercises. The sector will be working with PCIS, SLTTGCC, and other sectors in the coming year to identify and prioritize regional interdependencies that impact the communications infrastructure.

2.2 Collecting Infrastructure Information

Although information about the sector's architecture elements may be available, collecting information about network access architecture and functions at the customer level can present significant challenges. Monitoring customer use of the communications infrastructure is extremely difficult, particularly when customers move parts of their organization geographically, change the use of particular architecture elements as they are associated with particular missions, or merge with other organizations. The dynamic nature of communications technology further complicates the process. As a result, DHS and sector owners and operators must rely on each customer to identify customer-level critical assets.

CSSP infrastructure information falls into two categories: (1) architectural infrastructure information, and (2) specific infrastructure information.

Collecting Architectural Infrastructure Information

For the collection of architectural infrastructure information, NCS works with industry to examine sector infrastructure elements, including the backbone, signaling and control systems, shared assets and systems, access, and customer equipment. Understanding the changing nature of the Communications Sector is critical to identifying and validating sector architecture elements. Industry and government partners work closely to develop a deeper understanding of these architecture elements and their associated assets, systems, networks, and functions. This process also considers the dependencies and interdependencies of the architecture elements with physical and cyber/logical infrastructure not owned by the sector.

The Communications Sector has examined the architecture elements of each type of communications carrier (e.g., wireline, wireless, satellite, cable, and broadcasting) and has classified it into one of the proposed five major architecture element categories. As discussed in section 2.1, the Communications Sector identified asset/system categories within each architecture element, as well as their respective functions. The majority of the identified sector cyber/logical infrastructure falls into the signaling and control systems category; however, there are asset/system categories within the other elements.

Collecting Specific Infrastructure Information

Through well-established relationships with individual carriers, NCS requests specific asset information on an as-needed basis, particularly during incidents of national significance or in preparation for National Special Security Events (NSSEs). The NCC is the main industry POC for asset information. In response to requests for sector asset information by DHS, the NCC works with industry to clarify the instances in which asset information will be collected. The NCC periodically tests this process to ensure that procedures work in a timely manner. The NCC has developed a formal process through which the National Operations Center (NOC) works with the NCC to identify specific sector assets that are related to an explicit, credible threat during emergencies or in preparation for NSSEs. In these cases, the NCC may acquire relevant asset information from its industry members' corporate operations centers. The NCC then passes the information to the NOC and appropriate State and local agencies.

NCS collects asset information for the NCS Network Design and Analysis Capability (NDAC) through contractually obtained information and by using commercial and private databases, such as the Local Exchange Routing Guide (LERG). Communications Sector industry partners maintain stringent proprietary control over the dissemination of infrastructure-related information for competitive and security reasons. Based on a trusting and long-standing working relationship with NCS, however, industry partners traditionally have provided selected proprietary information directly to NCS on a case-by-case basis. As the Emergency Support Function 2 (ESF-2) lead, NCS has also created a deployable disaster communications asset database to assist in tracking assets for incident response. NCS uses this information for operational analysis, program development, and operations, and integrates some of the information into NDAC. Additionally, the NCS Government-Industry Planning and Management (GIP&M) Branch works with the NCC, the NCS Technology and Programs Branch, and sector partners to respond to requests for DHS infrastructure protection program asset criteria and data calls.

Regulatory Requirements

Federal regulatory requirements for providing infrastructure information in the sector vary by subsector. Currently, the FCC requires wireless and broadcasting infrastructure owners to file information on equipment location and type. Wireline infrastructure operators submit data annually to the FCC to allow for the measurement of competition and service quality. The information required in these filings includes a summary of infrastructure (e.g., the number of access lines), service quality, and financial data. Furthermore, the FCC requires wireline, wireless, cable, and satellite carriers to report network outages. The FCC maintains an expert staff of engineers and statisticians to analyze this data in an attempt to reveal troublesome trends in network reliability and security. For example, the FCC designs its reports to provide information on the extent to which industry best practices developed by CSRIC are being applied. The reports also include detailed information about the causes of network outages and the methods used to restore service. With this information in hand, the FCC works with industry bodies such as the Network Reliability Steering Committee (NRSC)[6] and CSRIC to improve communications reliability and security. It then documents the resulting improvements in revised or new best practices so that they can be applied more broadly across the industry.

2.3 Verifying Infrastructure Information

In addition to the procedures and processes employed by Communications Sector industry partners to verify the ongoing accuracy and completeness of their own infrastructure information, industry also participates in NCS efforts to maintain strong, trusted partnerships with various government agencies. The trust and productivity of these relationships require strong policies and procedures for collecting, handling, storing, and disseminating information; a common understanding of the ultimate use of that data; and a process for ensuring compliance and enforcement to protect the interests of the government and its private sector partners.

NCS verifies information through multiple sources, primarily through interviews with carriers. Each carrier verifies the asset and systems information and network topology that it controls. Such interviews may identify the need for more in-depth analysis by the carrier, in which case contractual relationships may be required to reimburse the carrier's cost. NCS addresses incomplete and incorrect information by reengaging the owners and operators of the related assets, systems, and networks to ensure that the information is accurate and comprehensive.

2.4 Updating Infrastructure Information

Maintenance of communications infrastructure databases is a continual effort undertaken by a host of sector partners. NCS updates collected information daily, monthly, quarterly, or annually, depending on the source of the information, licensing agreements, and contractual obligations. It also uses these sources to update infrastructure information. For the purposes of the DHS infrastructure protection program, NCS provides updates on data sets as permitted by the original owners of the data. The sector updates critical asset information via the annual Level 1/Level 2 data call program (see chapter 4 for more information).

---

6 The NRSC is a subcommittee of the Alliance for Telecommunications Industry Solutions, whose objective is to monitor and improve communications network reliability.

3. Assess Risks

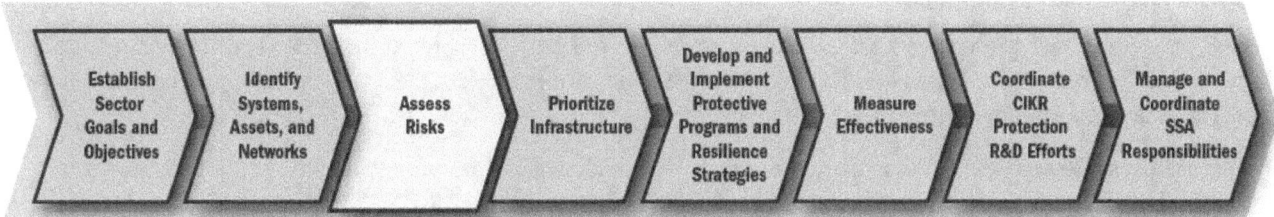

The approach to assessing the risk to the Communications Sector is based on the following statement from the NIPP: "Risk in the 21st century results from a complex mix of manmade and naturally occurring threats and hazards, including terrorist attacks, accidents, natural disasters, and other emergencies. Within this context, our CIKR may be directly exposed to the events themselves or indirectly exposed as a result of the dependencies and interdependencies among CIKR."[7]

3.1 Risk Assessment Overview

The Communications Sector faces both natural and manmade threats. The terrorist events of September 11th, as well as the unprecedented impact that Hurricane Katrina in 2005 and the Red River floods in the Upper Midwest in 2009 had on the communications infrastructure, have solidified the existence of a new all-hazards threat environment. While the sector risk assessments conducted to date conclude that degradation or disruption of a communications service does not directly lead to national impacts, these analyses also conclude that local and regional effects on communications may lead to national impacts. The impacts of local and regional events in the communications networks would not likely affect human life, but may harm the economy, public morale, or government capability. The severity of these impacts depends on the particular area disrupted and the network implementation and mission of the affected government and commercial end users.

Across the Communications Sector, risk assessments are an ongoing activity designed to include new asset and network configurations, as well as the evaluation of existing assets in light of new threats. This process is designed to examine any national, regional, and local impacts that could potentially affect overall national infrastructure resilience. Risk assessments include participation and feedback from government and industry partners.

Risk assessments will continue to capitalize on expertise from CSCC, CGCC, NSTAC, NCC, and NSIE members, as well as other partners. The primary role of industry partners is to analyze vulnerabilities related to the national communications architecture. Government partners provide threat information based on available intelligence and knowledge of critical government

---

[7] 2009 National Infrastructure Protection Plan.

dependencies. The government will continue to provide regional analyses for high-risk regions, including major facilities, dependencies, and associated connectivity. The government has overall responsibility for leading and coordinating all of the sponsored risk assessments. Industry and government jointly assess potential consequences as described in HSPD-7.

Risk Assessment Across the 18 CIKR Sectors

The NIPP views CIKR risk assessments as an integral part of a sector's comprehensive picture of its overall exposure to risk and as being key to the maintenance and enhancement of a sector's resilience and robustness. DHS HITRAC works with the 18 CIKR sectors to produce sector-specific threat assessments that provide an overall review of potential terrorist threats against the sector and an analysis of how these threats relate to sector vulnerabilities. These assessments include known specific and general terrorist threat information, as well as relevant background information, such as possible terrorist objectives and motives as they apply to the sector.

CSSP Risk Assessment Framework

The CSSP provides a strategic framework for the sector's partners to collaboratively protect the Nation's critical communications infrastructure. The framework is based on the goals of the CSSP and aims to increase the resilience of the Communications Sector. The basic goals of this effort are:

- **Resilient Infrastructure:** Critical infrastructure and their communications capabilities should be able to withstand natural or manmade hazards with minimal interruption or failure.

- **Diversity:** Facilities should have diverse primary and backup communications capabilities that do not share common points of failure.

- **Redundancy:** Facilities should use multiple communications capabilities to sustain business operations and eliminate single points of failure that could disrupt primary services.

- **Recoverability:** Plans and processes should be in place to restore operations quickly if an interruption or failure occurs.

The CSSP risk framework is summarized in the table provided below. Sector assessments are ongoing and are continually updated. NCS has the responsibility to coordinate all of the government-sponsored segments with all sector partners. The industry self-assessments are company specific and provide the basis for input from industry subject matter experts (SMEs).

Table 3-1: Summary of CSSP Risk Assessments

Industry Self-Assessments	Government-Sponsored Assessments		Government-Sponsored Cross-Sector Dependency Analyses
Internal Industry Assessments **Recognition:** Industry routinely conducts self-assessments as a part of its business operations. **Approach:** Owners and operators conduct self-assessments of their networks voluntarily.	**National Sector Risk Assessment (NSRA)** **Goal:** Examine Communications Sector architecture to identify national risks. **Approach:** Industry and government conduct a high-level qualitative risk analysis of the entire Communications Sector.	**Detailed Risk Assessments** **Goal:** Conduct detailed risk assessments on architecture elements that have been identified as being high risk by NSRA. **Approach:** Government works in conjunction with industry to conduct detailed quantitative assessments with respect to mission impact.	**Sector Dependency Assessments** **Goal:** Assist other sectors in the assessment of communications dependency for high-risk assets. **Approach:** Identify high-level critical sector communications dependencies and leverage NCS risk assessment methodologies to identify communications dependencies specific to a facility or function.

Industry Self-Assessments

The Communications Sector risk management approach focuses on resilience, service reliability, response, and recovery. Risk assessment and management processes are, by nature, customer driven; owners and operators must offer reliable service and quickly respond to and restore service when an outage occurs. However, the diverse nature of the communications industry, including wireless, wireline, satellite, cable, and broadcasting, makes the creation of a common methodology for self-assessments impractical. As with engineering and operational activities, specific risk management methodologies used by companies are closely guarded. In general, changes to systems, processes, facilities, and the environment can have an impact on the level of security. Industry self-assessments are conducted to verify compliance with policies, standards, contracts, and regulations.

Cross-Sector Dependency Analyses

Consequence, and therefore risk, cannot be accurately determined without considering what functions or services a particular asset, system, or network supports, and the availability of those functions or services to the user. This is especially true for the Communications Sector, which is one of four sectors that the NIPP describes as potentially impacting all other sectors. Thus, interdependencies between the Communications Sector and the other sectors are extremely important to identify.

Based on the importance of these interdependencies, the Communications Sector determined that it would focus a portion of its risk assessment strategy on cross-sector dependency analysis. For high-risk CIKR, NCS and government and industry partners will continue to facilitate communications dependency analyses for other critical infrastructure sectors by performing assessments that evaluate facilities' communications resilience. These dependency analyses require the participation of the other SSAs, State and local governments, and relevant industry partners from the Communications Sector and the other critical infrastructure sectors. The results provide an assessment of risk and suggested mitigation options.

NCS-Sponsored Risk Assessment Efforts

Originally published in May 2007, the CSSP provides a framework for industry and government partners to establish a coordinated strategy to protect the Nation's critical communications infrastructure. Part of this framework includes conducting national risk assessments. The baseline assessment, entitled National Sector Risk Assessment (NSRA), was conducted in 2008. The NSRA identified high-level nationally critical architecture elements.

NCS followed up the NSRA with a cross-sector study that is addressed in the CDEP report. The study (described below) examined the potential impact of long-term power outages on the Communications Sector.

National Sector Risk Assessment

The NSRA for the Communications Sector was completed and published in April 2008. It comprehensively evaluated the Communications Sector's exposure to risk by analyzing the three factors that the NIPP uses to define risk: threats, vulnerabilities, and consequences. The sector recognizes the NSRA as a major achievement because it met the risk-based analysis requested by the NIPP and the CSSP and created a methodology to serve as a provisional foundation for future analyses within the Communications Sector. The assessment considered the diverse technologies that make up the infrastructure, including wireline, wireless, satellite, cable, and broadcasting.

In 2010, the NSRA will be updated. Recommendations from the 2008 NSRA, which includes the analysis of the risks associated with global communications infrastructure and how the risk profile might change as a result of coordinated multiple attacks, will be considered. In addition, the 2010 effort will include expansion and continuation of the analysis of cross-sector dependencies with the other 17 CIKR sectors.

The 2010 NSRA will utilize Federal Government representatives from the CGCC and industry representatives from CSCC as part of the working group that will scope, design, and complete the new risk assessment. The 2008 NSRA contained two overarching assessments:

- A risk assessment of physical and human threats to communications infrastructure; and

- A risk assessment of cyber threats to communications infrastructure.

The 2010 risk assessment will use the 2008 NSRA methodology as a baseline. The Communications Sector used the following risk assessment framework to evaluate and produce the 2008 NSRA:

Consequence measures the cost or impact of an incident, which will be measured based on impact on human life and well-being, the economy, public confidence, and government's ability to function;

Vulnerability assessments estimate the odds that a characteristic of, or flaw in, an infrastructure element could make it susceptible to destruction, disruption, or exploitation based on its design, location, security posture, processes, or operations; and

Threat considers the intent or capability of an adversary for a terrorist threat or the probability of occurrence for a natural disaster or accident.

Communications NSRA Assumptions and Constraints

The 2010 NSRA working group will consider the 2008 NSRA assumptions and constraints in the risk assessment implementation. The 2008 NSRA considered the following:

Single incidents from the Strategic Homeland Infrastructure Risk Assessment (SHIRA) and FEMA: The NSRA is limited to threats included in lists from SHIRA in 2007 and FEMA's National Planning Scenarios. These threat lists include single incidents (i.e., a single attack, accident, or natural disaster), such as hurricanes, earthquakes, floods, explosive attacks; biological, chemical, and radiological attacks; and cyber attacks.

Focus on functional areas: This analysis did not address individual assets (i.e., a physical address or a particular switch), but is a representative analysis focused on functional areas (i.e., general elements and asset classes). Individual assets are generally not nationally critical in and of themselves due to the sector's built-in resilience.

Only domestic public networks: This analysis includes only those architecture elements within the public networks of the United States that are owned and operated by service providers.

Direct consequence focus: This assessment identifies the direct consequences of loss or disruption of communications services (i.e., how the loss or disruption of various communications services affects national communications).

Network modeling: The NSRA did not incorporate network modeling, which would evaluate the impact on other sectors.

Conclusions and Recommendations

For physical, cyber, and human events, the 2008 NSRA analysis presents two major findings when considering national impacts (e.g., human life, economic, public confidence, and government capability) resulting from impaired or disrupted communications or damaged communications infrastructure. Within the constraints of the NSRA (a single event), the results confirmed the following:

Degradation or disruption of a communications service does not directly lead to national impacts. Consequences are dependent on how user missions (industry or government) rely on communications services.

The communications network does not have to be nationally degraded or disrupted to cause national impacts. For example, a limited local outage could result in national impacts if a key government or commercial user, who is extremely dependent on the communications network, is affected and the nature of the effects lead to significant impacts.

The report also concludes that the risk of disruption from a single cyber attack is greater than the risk from a single physical attack.

The CDEP Report

The impetus for this cross-sector analysis came from challenges revealed in after-action reports that followed natural disasters and incidents such as the 2003 Northeast Blackout. Studies revealed a potential vulnerability concerning the interdependencies between the Communications and Energy Sectors in the event of a long-term outage. To address this vulnerability, NSTAC commissioned an industry led examination of these dependencies, leading to the recommendations made in the NSTAC Report to the President on Telecommunications and Electric Power Interdependencies: The Implications of Long-Term Outages (hereinafter referred to as the TEPI report). In response to the issues raised in the TEPI report, the NCS Committee of Principals (COP) established the CDEP Working Group (CDEPWG) in 2007 to address the TEPI report's recommendations as they pertained to NS/EP communications, as well as the broad range of issues resulting from the Communications Sector's dependence on the Energy Sector.

The Communications Sector is reviewing the CDEP report and implementing selected recommendations with assistance from the CGCC in a new working group. By combining CGCC knowledge and expertise with that of industry representatives from the CSCC to implement recommendations, the long-term power outage risk to the Communications Sector will be reduced. The working group is implementing a major recommendation that it is important for the Communications and Energy Sectors to work together to develop strategies to address the impact of a long-term outage event. Future activities may include a quantitative risk assessment and the investigation of backup/alternative power solutions.

3.2 Screening Infrastructure

Communications Sector risk assessments will begin by defining the communications architecture to create an overall model of the sector elements. The NSRA model included the services; core network; signaling and databases; operations management; and access segments of broadcast, cable, satellite, wireless, and wireline. The following process occurs within the model:

- End users first connect to an access network.
- Each access network then connects to the core network.
- The core network provides nationwide interconnectivity among the access networks and their respective end users and access to international gateways, allowing end users to communicate with end users in other countries.

As noted previously, a risk assessment should address three components: consequence, vulnerability, and threat. The following subsections describe how each component will be addressed as part of the government-sponsored risk assessment process.

3.3 Assessing Consequences

Consequence measures the cost or impact of an incident, which will be measured based on the impact on human life and well-being, the economy, public confidence, and the government's ability to function.

Consequence assessments narrow the scope of the risk assessment process to those missions having the greatest impact if disrupted, destroyed, or exploited. The 2008 NSRA included an evaluation of the dependencies and interdependencies of the sector's physical and cyber architecture elements. It narrowed the scope of sector risk assessments to mission impact that was nationally critical. National criticality is based on the consequences of primary concern to the Communications Sector. These concerns are also the focus of the NCS operational analysis process, which assesses the impact of an incident on the Nation's communications infrastructure.

Table 3-2: Communications Sector Consequences of Concern

HSPD-7 Consequence	Consequences of Primary Concern to Communications Sector
Human Impact: Effects on human life and physical well-being (e.g., fatalities and injuries)	Emergency communications (e.g., public safety answering points (PSAPs), first responders) Hospitals and other public health facilities
Economic Impact: Direct and indirect effects on the economy	Financial markets Communications supporting CIKR response and recovery (e.g., transportation, electric power) Core network and Internet backbone (national communications connectivity) Distributed control systems
Impact on Public Confidence: Effects on public morale and confidence in national economic and political institutions	Communications supporting CIKR response and recovery Core network and Internet backbone (national communications connectivity)
Impact on Government Capabilities: Effects on the government's ability to maintain order, deliver minimum essential public services, ensure public health and safety, and carry out national security-related missions	NS/EP communications Continuity of Operations (COOP)/Continuity of Government (COG) communications Law enforcement communications

The 2010 NSRA will consider the 2008 NSRA's major findings when reviewing national impacts. The new assessment will review whether access segments are still at an elevated risk and have the potential to cause national impacts if degraded. It will also review whether the impacts would still be focused on the particular customers within the geographical area, their mission reliance on communications, and their specific communications architecture.

The 2010 NSRA will ultimately update whether potential national impacts are still difficult to assess and cannot be determined by typical metrics, such as traffic volume or number of customers.

3.4 Assessing Vulnerabilities

Vulnerability assessments estimate the odds that a characteristic of, or flaw in, an infrastructure element could make it susceptible to destruction, disruption, or exploitation based on its design, location, security posture, processes, or operations. Vulnerabilities typically are identified through internal assessments and information sharing with customers, vendors, and suppliers.

A vulnerability assessment methodology was developed as part of the complete CSSP risk assessment methodology. The methodology examined physical, cyber, and human vulnerabilities and considered relevant national preparedness threat scenarios. The process varied depending on the architecture elements being studied and included SME interviews, site visits, and modeling and analysis.

The vulnerabilities of communications architecture elements may vary depending on whether they are operational or implementation specific. Operational vulnerabilities may include those that result from the inherent principles of network design, unanticipated network congestion caused by external factors, or collateral consequences from major disasters or events. Implementation-specific vulnerabilities may be very particular in nature—from bugs in application software and protocol deficiencies to backdoors in vendor equipment firmware or software. The magnitude of the implementation vulnerabilities also varies depending on the exposure of the vulnerable equipment. While embedded firmware, for example, may have only limited exposure to configuration and maintenance functions, systems such as the Domain Name Service require a high degree of exposure in order to provide service to customers.

3.5 Assessing Threats

Threat considers the intent or capability of an adversary with regard to a terrorist attack or the probability of occurrence for a natural disaster or accident. HITRAC conducts sector threat assessments and integrated threat analyses for all CIKR sectors, bringing together intelligence and infrastructure specialists to ensure a complete understanding of the risks to U.S. CIKR. HITRAC works in partnership with the U.S. intelligence and law enforcement communities to integrate and analyze available threat information. HITRAC also partners with the SSAs and owners and operators to ensure that their expertise on infrastructure operations is integrated into threat analysis. Threat assessments also are conducted through public-private partnerships such as NSIEs and the C-ISAC.

NCS will continue to use HITRAC to support the production of attack-specific threat scenarios. The scenarios are detailed vignettes of specific methods, techniques, and actions that terrorists are likely to use to attack specific types of U.S. CIKR. The scenarios are based on HITRAC analysis of known terrorist capabilities or on their stated intents as derived from intelligence and the study of terrorist tactics, techniques, and capabilities. Threat scenarios are specific enough to be used by corporate or facility security officers to support operational security planning.

The sector threat assessment produced by HITRAC identified few direct threats and vulnerabilities. With relatively few attacks to communications facilities or infrastructure worldwide, the threat to the Communications Sector is low. However, the risk for the sector as a residual target is high because of the sector's interdependencies with other critical infrastructure.

HITRAC also produced a cyber threat assessment. The assessment concluded that cyber/logical vulnerabilities are compounded by today's dynamic business environment, which is characterized by reliance on open-system protocols and commercial off-the-shelf products to manage networks, and the interconnection of management networks through the Internet and with enterprise networks. Specific categories of cyber-related threats include the following: hacking, cyber warfare (e.g., modular malicious code, bot networks, phishing, etc.), outsourcing, "hacktivists," and insider threat.

Cyber Threats

NCS works with NCSD and US-CERT to understand cyber threats. Similar to a physical threat, the source of a cyber incident may be local, regional, national, or international. However, a cyber incident is different because it can be launched from anywhere, at any time, and against any network. Threats range from random hackers, to criminals, to sophisticated nation-state adversaries. Nonmalicious acts (physical or cyber) may impact the Communications Sector as well. Single cyber attacks or accidents are considered to be attacks initiated from a single source, although the incident may be directed at or affect multiple targets. Therefore, the Communications Sector will promote redundancy and create best practices guidance to provide education and awareness for owners and operators of communications infrastructure.

4. Prioritize Infrastructure

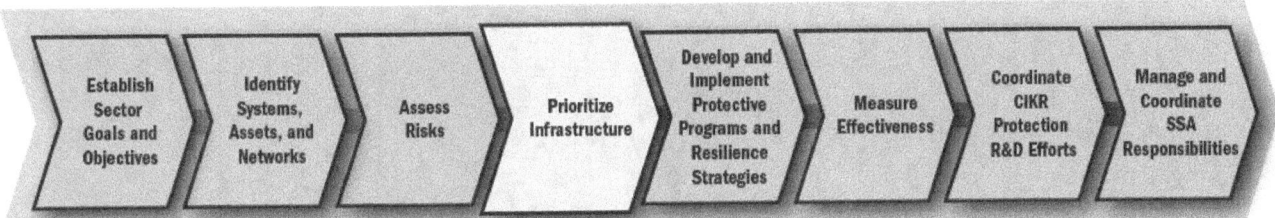

To ensure that resources are directed toward protecting the country's infrastructure, the Communications Sector needs to normalize and prioritize assets, systems, and networks to the maximum extent possible; this is also the case across all other sectors. This chapter focuses on the process that the Communications Sector uses to calculate and normalize risk assessment results in a way that can be compared with other sectors and then prioritizes the infrastructure for the purposes of protective program requirements.

4.1 Communications Architecture Prioritization

DHS HITRAC conducts integrated threat analysis for all CIKR sectors. As called for in section 201 of the Homeland Security Act, HITRAC brings together intelligence and infrastructure specialists to ensure a complete and sophisticated understanding of the risks to U.S. CIKR. HITRAC works in partnership with the U.S. Intelligence Community and law enforcement to integrate and analyze intelligence and law enforcement information on threats. It also works in partnership with the SSAs and owners and operators to ensure that their expertise on infrastructure operations is integrated into threat analyses. This coordination is carried out through a number of mechanisms, including the use of liaison personnel from the private sector, the use of on-call SMEs, and coordination with existing organizations such as the NCC, SCCs, and ISACs.

A critical element of that process is prioritization. The current prioritization process primarily considers consequence-related metrics and functions performed by a particular asset, system, or network to determine criticality. As the risk assessment process has matured and ample data has been collected, the Communications Sector is moving toward a process that prioritizes infrastructure based on the results of the full risk assessment process.

Migration to a Risk-Based Prioritization Process

For fiscal year (FY) 2010, HITRAC made changes to improve the transparency of the process, and the defensibility and utility of the resulting lists of CIKR. The historic process and methodology were based on two tiers that used distinct criteria. These criteria were:

- **Tier 1 Assets.** Infrastructure whose disruption would cause two of four consequences on a list that HITRAC had developed from prior analysis of threats and potential consequences; and

- **Tier 2 Assets.** Capacity-based criteria developed by each infrastructure sector.

The new system for prioritization represents growth and maturity in HITRAC's work with the CIKR sectors. It also is the product of analysis performed through partnerships between industry and government to properly characterize the sector to improve sector protection.

During an incident, communications infrastructure elements are now categorized as critical based on incident location and the specific effects on end users in the incident impact area. As an example, during Hurricane Rita, many of the Communication Sector's assets, systems, and networks in the regional area would not have been on the prioritized list using the prior method. However, many of the assets in the area were critical to the economy for the region and the country. The new prioritization method allows for more flexibility. To determine which assets, systems, and networks are most critical during situational impact analyses, infrastructure elements supporting the following missions were identified:

- NS/EP;

- COOP/COG missions;

- Public health and safety (e.g., PSAPs, hospitals);

- Law enforcement;

- Core network/IP backbone (i.e., national communications connectivity);

- Financial markets; and

- CIKR supporting response/recovery (e.g., transportation, electric power).

The Communications Sector is now focusing its risk assessments on communications architecture elements rather than specific assets, systems, and networks. In 2010, HITRAC's methodology moved from attribute-based criteria to consequence-based criteria. HITRAC solicits infrastructure nominations from sectors and States during an annual data call. Sectors and States are given the opportunity to request reconsideration of any nomination(s) that are rejected because they do not appear to meet the required criteria. The former Tier 1 and Tier 2 categories have been replaced by Level 1 and Level 2.

The Level 1 and Level 2 lists include infrastructure capable of sustaining "national or regional catastrophic effects." The lists will still be developed through a national data call involving sector and State infrastructure protection partners. Sector lists of infrastructure, populated by the SSAs, will include Level 1 and Level 2 infrastructure, as well as infrastructure critical to a specific sector. State specific lists of critical infrastructure include the Level 1, Level 2, and Sector list infrastructure, as well as infrastructure critical to the State. This list will be populated by the State HSAs. Foreign lists will include foreign infrastructure critical to the Nation's public health, economy, and national security. Items on this list will be identified through a national data call involving the Intelligence Community and sector and State partners. Figure 4-1 depicts the FY 2010 "Lists of Lists" approach.

At the conclusion of a risk assessment, NCS will validate the corresponding entries to HITRAC and will make the appropriate updates to allow DHS to work with owners and operators to develop and implement appropriate protective measures.

During incidents, industry and government work together through the NCC to identify priorities for restoration and provisioning. The FCC Telecommunications Service Priority (TSP) Report and Order (FCC 88-341) dictates priorities for circuits that are registered as critical for NS/EP communications.

Industry Self-Prioritization

The diverse nature of the communications industry complicates the creation of a common methodology for prioritization. Companies independently determine what constitutes the appropriate priority of their assets relative to their own needs and circumstances. Companies need to adopt or employ practices based on their factual situations, the practicality and effectiveness of particular actions, and economic and technological feasibility. In making this determination, companies consider all information that might be relevant. Companies also consult with legal counsel to ascertain whether their actions comply with relevant Federal, State, and local laws, which vary by the type of communications company. For example, as part of the business continuity and business impact analysis function, owners and operators routinely assess which aspects of the business are essential for determining levels of resilience in the event of a manmade or natural disaster. However, how a company gets to this point and what is considered to be critical will vary by company.

Cross-Sector Interdependency Analysis

As part of the 2010 National Sector Risk Assessment, NCS will lead a cross-sector interdependency analysis with its sector partners. Using common scales for consequences, vulnerabilities, threats, and overall risk can normalize the results of these assessments and enable their comparison across sectors to the extent possible. Because the DHS-provided risk assessment methods/tools are not always suitable as is for the Communications Sector, NCS will work closely with DHS and will collaborate with the CSCC to determine methods for assigning qualitative and quantitative ratings.

The centralized normalization process performed by DHS will allow for further evaluation of cross-sector interdependencies. This is important because SSAs often do not have the data to assess consequences accurately based on these interdependencies, which, in turn, can affect overall risk. To assist in this process, DHS will collaborate with the Communications Sector to develop a general list of interdependencies with other sectors—an effort that NCS has begun with the development of the sample list shown in figure 4-1. When requested, NCS also will assist DHS and the National Infrastructure Simulation and Analysis Center (NISAC) with cross-sector interdependency analyses, reaching out to additional Communications Sector partners as appropriate.

4.2 The Prioritization Process

NCS participates in the DHS National Critical Infrastructure Prioritization Program (NCIPP). Prioritized lists are developed through an annual data call using criteria developed by HITRAC for the NCIPP. NCIPP identifies both domestic and foreign "too critical to fail" infrastructure, which are then used to inform homeland security grant programs and other critical infrastructure protection activities.

Prioritization of Communications Assets, Systems, and Networks

The Communications Sector List

NCS manages the Communications Sector List. The list is designed to include assets, systems, and networks. There are four types of components to the list:

- Nominations submitted through NCS/NCC;
- Analytical cross-sector communications dependencies;
- Nominated emergency services; and
- High-capacity assets of record.

The following entities will make submissions to the list:

1. **Industry.** The private sector will designate those facilities that are critical to their networks. Private sector participants will include:

   – C-ISAC members (includes wireline, wireless, satellite, broadcast, cable, and networks supporting cyberspace);[8]

   – Other industry input offering public services (non-C-ISAC members); and

   – Industry partners who support systems that enhance communications or are highly dependent on communications for the delivery of services (e.g., Global Positioning System (GPS), Air Traffic Control Network).

2. **Manager/Director of NCS.** The Manager/Director of NCS will work with HITRAC to identify additional assets of interest.

3. **NCS Committee of Principals (COP)/Council of Representatives (COR).** COP/COR will designate government assets or operations that are mission critical, essential, and/or that enhance communications.

4. **Cross-Sector Communications Dependencies.** The Communications Sector uses the combined cross-sector lists of Level 1 and Level 2 CIKR to determine supporting communications facilities:

   – Three or more Level 1/Level 2 CIKR through one communications facility;

   – Nominated communications assets that are specific to a CIKR asset, as designated by the sector (e.g., Level 1 CIKR).

5. **Emergency Services.** Emergency services include PSAPs and the Emergency Alert System (EAS) that have been nominated by the FCC, the Protective Security Advisors (PSAs), and ESF-2 communications representatives. Nominations will be coordinated with Emergency Services Sector and other Communications Sector representatives. These criteria will include the following:

   – PSAPs should be registered with the FCC, including single jurisdiction, multiple jurisdiction, and consolidated PSAPs, as described in National Emergency Number Association (NENA) Minimum Standards for Emergency Telephone Notification Systems Document 56-003, June 12, 2004;

   – PSAPs should be located in areas of persistent critical impact; and

   – The service should provide unique capabilities (e.g., a non-English broadcast of EAS information in areas with high concentrations of non-English-speaking individuals).

6. **High-Capacity Assets.** High-capacity assets include:

   – Major switching centers;

   – Major underwater cable landings; and

   – Telecommunications hotels that are deemed to provide critical mission support on a regional or national scale.

7. **Automatic Inclusion.** Credible threats and national security implications are automatically included on the prioritization list for protection.

---

[8] *Cyberspace is defined as "a global domain within the information environment consisting of the interdependent network of information technology infrastructure, including the Internet, telecommunications networks, computer systems, and embedded processors and controllers" (National Security Presidential Directive 54/ Homeland Security Presidential Directive 23, Cyber Security Policy, January 8, 2008).*

Figure 4-1: The "List of Lists" Approach

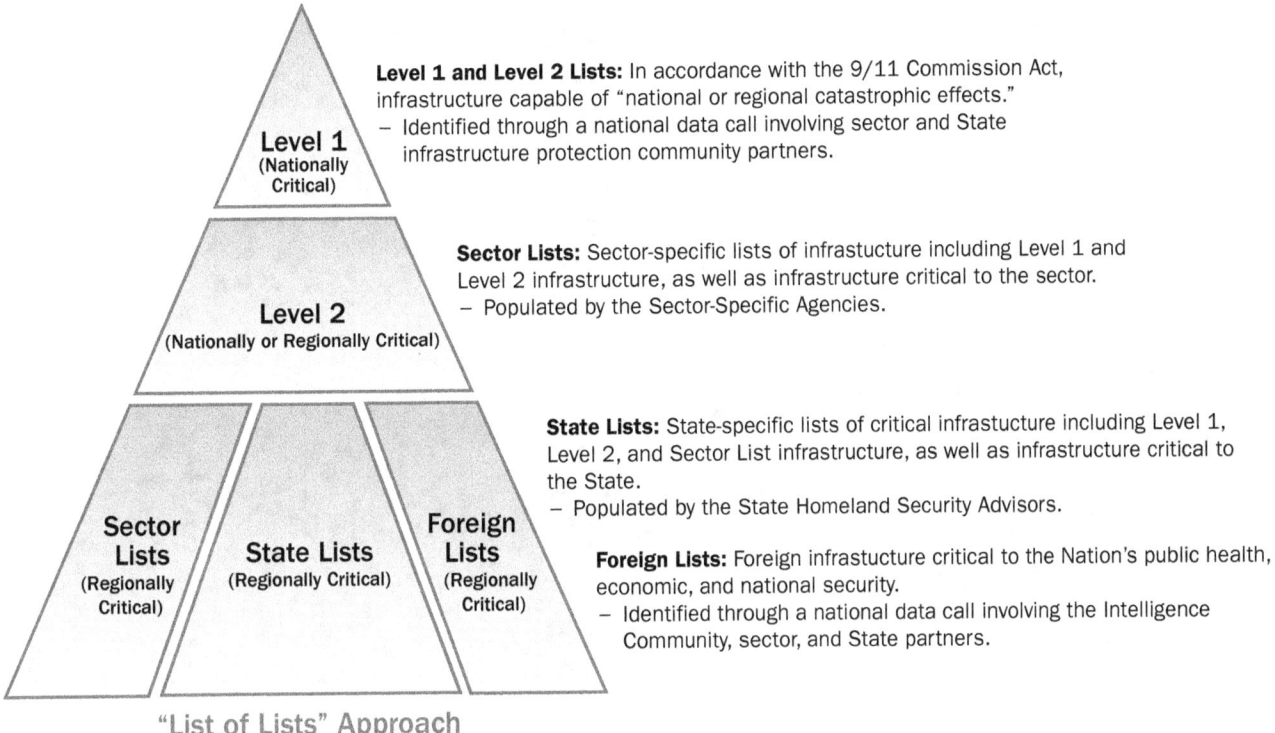

Level 1 and Level 2 Lists: In accordance with the 9/11 Commission Act, infrastructure capable of "national or regional catastrophic effects."
– Identified through a national data call involving sector and State infrastructure protection community partners.

Sector Lists: Sector-specific lists of infrastucture including Level 1 and Level 2 infrastructure, as well as infrastructure critical to the sector.
– Populated by the Sector-Specific Agencies.

State Lists: State-specific lists of critical infrastucture including Level 1, Level 2, and Sector List infrastructure, as well as infrastructure critical to the State.
– Populated by the State Homeland Security Advisors.

Foreign Lists: Foreign infrastucture critical to the Nation's public health, economic, and national security.
– Identified through a national data call involving the Intelligence Community, sector, and State partners.

"List of Lists" Approach

Prioritization of Cyber Assets, Systems, and Networks

NCS, as the Communications Sector SSA, works with its Communications Sector partners and DHS NCSD on communications cybersecurity planning. NCSD is the SSA for the IT Sector and is responsible for working with sector partners from all 18 CIKR sectors to assist in prioritizing cyber assets, systems, and networks.

5. Develop and Implement Protective Programs and Resilience Strategies

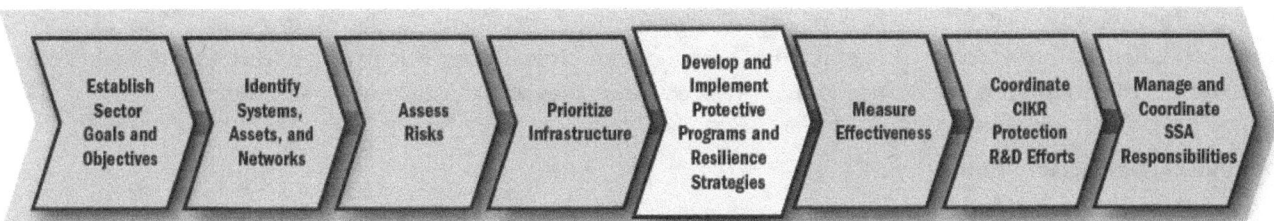

This chapter presents an overview of the sector strategy and processes for developing and implementing protective programs and resilience strategies. It takes into account the sector's mature set of protective measures and partnerships, including various government initiatives, as well as those that have been put in place by industry. It also provides a roadmap for growth in the partnership and improvements to existing programs.

5.1 Overview of Sector Protective Programs and Resilience Strategies

The Communications Sector's security strategy is to focus on ensuring that the Nation's communications systems and networks are secure, resilient, and rapidly restored after an incident. The three Communications Sector goals outlined in chapter 1 reflect the common viewpoint among sector partners that allows a collective approach to developing protective programs and resilience strategies.

The Communications Sector, through an established self-management process, is responsible for supporting numerous protective programs that are either sponsored by or owned by government entities. The existing protective programs:

• Help stakeholders prepare for crisis situations, alerting them of potential problems/attacks;

• Mitigate vulnerabilities;

• Provide priority communications services;

• Facilitate the recovery of critical communications assets for Federal, State, local, and tribal governments; and

• Address interdependencies with other sectors.

Communications Sector partners are working together to ensure that no single incident presents a substantial risk to the national communications infrastructure. Sector partners are addressing potential single point-of-failure issues through mechanisms that promote resilience and redundancy of the core network, signaling and databases, and operations, as well as programs to restore continuity through alternate systems and to speed restoration of communications when outages occur.

A continuously improving partnership will help industry and government prevent and prepare for a potential incident; detect a potential attack on the sector; mitigate the impact and/or respond to a major disruption to critical communications services; and recover and restore essential communications assets, services, and infrastructure after natural disasters and other incidents.

In the Communications Sector, the most effective protective programs are implemented by infrastructure owners and government in a cooperative partnership. Infrastructure owners, following proven business continuity and contingency planning practices, are responsible for protecting their corporate, physical, and internal assets. To protect those assets during either man-made or natural disasters, infrastructure owners must be provided with a thorough and accurate picture of the threat; possess a clear understanding of government infrastructure protection and recovery priorities; coordinate with the Federal Government, when necessary, to obtain the necessary resources and assistance related to the protection, sheltering, and credentialing of employees and access to fuel and energy sources; and have the ability to restore the sector without the constraints of overly burdensome regulations and governmental requirements and procedures that delay recovery efforts.

Government relies on infrastructure owners to share accurate information in a timely manner, provide access to architecture data, and provide assistance in restoring or reconstituting critical systems as response partners. Additionally, government depends on infrastructure owners to use best practices for critical infrastructure protection and resilience and to developed multilayered security programs that provide awareness and education programs to employees and customers.

Communications Sector Strategy

DHS is the executive agent for NCS. NCS has numerous programs that align with DHS national infrastructure protection strategies. NCS is responsible for coordinating the reduction of risk for the Communications Sector under HSPD-7; this coordination is managed by the DHS Office of Infrastructure Protection. This steady-state planning spans the spectrum of protective and preparedness activities and is an extension of the DHS risk management framework, as well as the national vision for a unified response posture.

NCS is also the co-lead for ESF-2 (Communications) with FEMA. Through the management of the NCC, NCS and private sector partners coordinate the response to significant sector disruption and manage recovery efforts under the National Response Framework (NRF).

OEC develops and manages the National Emergency Communications Plan (NECP). OEC oversees several programs for improving emergency communications for Federal, State, and local agencies, including ECPC, OEC ICTAP, and the SAFECOM program (excluding its RDT&E and standards functions). NECP serves as a strategic roadmap to help drive measurable improvements in the areas of interoperability, operability, and continuity of communications for emergency responders across the Nation.

The FCC provides regulatory and oversight functions. Additionally, it provides priority services outreach activities to ensure that critical NS/EP circuits are registered with TSP and that key officials have access to the Government Emergency Telecommunications Service (GETS) and the Wireless Priority Service (WPS).

These programs are focused largely on preparedness, response, and recovery measures within the Communications Sector. The continued success and evolution of these programs will help to ensure the security of the communications infrastructure and the delivery of services.

Resilience

According to the FCC, the elements of resilience include the ability of operable systems to recover from mishap, change, misfortune, or variation in mission or operating requirements. The following principles are elements of resilience: redundancy (multiplicity, spares); diversity (multiple routes, multiple suppliers); agility (ability to shift and move quickly); adaptability (ability to rapidly readjust); prioritization (utilizing dedicated or shared resources); geography (diversity, proximity); hardening (against force, natural disaster, electromagnetic pulse); and security (both cybersecurity and physical security). Resilience also refers to the ability of the system to evolve and advance as new technologies or capabilities are developed.

Per the NIPP, critical infrastructure sectors are responsible for achieving communications resilience by having an appropriate mix of diversity, redundancy, and recoverability based on a risk cost-benefit assessment. When performing resilience assessments, it is important to consider a number of factors, including:

- Essential business functions;
- Time sensitivity of each essential function;
- Threats to the continuity of the functions and the services on which they depend;
- Threat mitigation options;
- Cost-benefit analysis;
- Mitigation strategy;
- Implementation;
- Testing; and
- Information sharing.

National Security and Emergency Preparedness

NCS manages numerous industry and government developed and operated protective programs that further reduce the risk to the Communications Sector by ensuring the security of the communications infrastructure and the delivery of NS/EP communications services, with a strong focus on response and recovery. NCS partners with Federal departments and agencies to provide advice and recommendations to the Executive Office of the President (EOP) on NS/EP communications.

FEMA Disaster Emergency Communications (DEC) offices in the 10 Federal regions focus on planning, training, and exercising the restoration of short-term recovery solutions for communications at the Federal, State, and local levels. FEMA's field role is supported by significant field-deployable assets that are used to reestablish temporary wireline and wireless communications, as well as local emergency communications. FEMA does not manage industry relationships nor does FEMA coordinate long-term provisioning.

Continuity of Government

National Security Presidential Directive (NSPD) 51/HSPD-20 established a comprehensive program designed to ensure the survival of the Nation's constitutional form of government and the continuation of the performance of national essential functions (NEFs) under all conditions. The manager of NCS coordinates the publication of all communications capabilities that are required by this directive, conducts testing and develops a quarterly compliance report on the communications requirements, and annually develops recommended updates to the set of minimum continuity communications requirements for consideration by the NCS COP and by DHS.

Business Continuity Planning

Business continuity planning (BCP) is designed to assess and mitigate threats to the continuation of a communications company's business. A business continuity plan often entails planned processes and procedures beyond basic disaster recovery. It first analyzes threats to a company's infrastructure and seeks to build enough resilience to absorb most attacks or breakdowns without diminishing or seriously degrading communication services delivery. BCP next serves to manage events, whether they are natural catastrophes, manmade disasters, or other emergency situations, to ensure a company's survivability. BCP ensures that in the event of an interruption, an organization's entire infrastructure and all of its critical processes can continue to function.

Development of International Standards

In accordance with E.O. 12472 as amended, NCS works with voluntary consensus standards development organizations, both nationally and internationally, to ensure that evolving standards support NS/EP priority service NGN requirements and contribute technical recommendations to satisfy those requirements. NCS represents DHS and the United States as the technical representative and as the head of U.S. delegations at international communications technical standards meetings.

Implementation Overview

The protective program development and implementation process builds on sector goals and objectives, and their affiliated and prioritized high-risk infrastructure, as determined by the processes described in previous chapters. Government-sponsored protective programs enable industry to better collaborate to address issues that it normally would not address collectively due to competitive reasons. Protective programs will be linked directly to goals and related risks. Protective programs that currently operate to mitigate that risk include a set of priority communications programs geared toward the NS/EP user group. Companies also mitigate this risk through the network design processes.

The protective program development and implementation process will ensure that government protective programs are logically linked to specific goals and critical risks in order to justify costs. Industry is encouraged to undertake similar processes to justify its protective programs.

Importance of Communications for Federal, State, and Local Partners

Government officials, emergency responders, and public safety officials at all levels of government—Federal, State, local, and tribal—need seamless communications to accomplish their day-to-day missions and facilitate coordination of response efforts to natural disasters and manmade incidents. COG and COOP planning could demand immediate telecommunications restoration or long-term alternate communications connectivity as the result of an emergency, disaster, or evacuation incident. The need to communicate and share information among emergency response providers in real time is critical to managing emergency incidents, establishing command and control, sharing event situational awareness, and developing a common operating picture across a broad scale of incidents.

States also have protective program responsibilities for the Communications Sector. Current multi-State initiatives include development of not only multi-sector, multi-State access and credentialing procedures, but also of POC networks to be used for incident management.

NCS-Managed Protection and Resilience Programs

NCS manages and will continue to develop the following priority programs to reduce the impact of network congestion, improve access, and expedite restoration or provision of service for NS/EP users:

The Government Emergency Telecommunications Service (GETS) provides emergency access and priority processing in the local and long-distance segments of the PSTN. This service increases the likelihood that NS/EP personnel can complete critical calls during periods of PSTN disruption and congestion resulting from natural or manmade disasters. GETS uses three major types of networks: local networks, major long-distance networks, and government-leased networks.

The Wireless Priority Service (WPS) helps to ensure that key NS/EP personnel can complete critical calls by providing priority access during times of wireless network congestion to key leaders and supporting first responders. WPS provides priority commercial mobile radio service during and after emergencies for NS/EP personnel by ensuring that WPS calls receive the next available radio channel during times of wireless congestion.

The Telecommunications Service Priority (TSP) Program provides the regulatory, administrative, and operational framework for priority restoration and provision of NS/EP communication circuits in an emergency. Eligibility for the TSP program extends to Federal, State, and local governments; private industry; and foreign governments that have communications services that support an NS/EP mission. NCS is currently pursuing implementation of an NSTAC recommendation[9] to enhance the TSP program to accommodate requests from NS/EP users of wireless telecommunications services at critical sites.

The Next-Generation Priority Service (NGPS) is being developed by government and its industry partners. This technology will provide priority service capabilities over the Internet, standardize the technology across the industry through the commercial standards process, and ensure current priority service work into the future.

The NCS Internet Analysis Capability (IAC) identifies the infrastructure and assets of the organizations that make up the Internet, as well as the specific dependence that NS/EP programs and government agencies place on these assets for mission support. IAC software resources include a suite of in-house developed and commercial off-the-shelf analysis tools that draw from a mix of open-source, third-party, and proprietary data sets and are used to visualize network topologies, assess network performance, and identify and assess the risks to the Internet's logical networks or physical assets.

The NCS Network Design and Analysis Capability (NDAC) analyzes the different operational aspects of communications networks, such as the PSTN, under various stress conditions. NDAC software resources include the tools, models, and communications databases used to assess network performance, perform modeling and simulation, and visualize network topologies.

NCS Directive 3-10 describes the minimum requirements for continuity communications that enable Federal departments and agencies to execute their MEFs. NSPD-51/HSPD-20 established a comprehensive program designed to ensure the survival of our constitutional form of government and the continuation of the performance of NEFs under all conditions. The Office of the Manager of NCS coordinates publishing of all communications capabilities required by this directive; conducts testing and develops a quarterly compliance report on the communications requirements; and annually develops recommended updates to the set of minimum continuity communications requirements for consideration by the NCS COP and the DHS Executive Agent. This program centers on the integration of three fundamental policy concepts: Enduring Constitutional Government (ECG), COG, and COOP.

Emergency Support Function 2 (ESF-2) supports the restoration of the communications infrastructure, facilitates the recovery of systems and applications from cyber attacks, and coordinates Federal communications support for response efforts during incidents that require a coordinated Federal response. ESF-2 implements the provisions of the Office of Science and Technology Policy (OSTP) National Plan for Telecommunications Support in Non-Wartime Emergencies (NPTS). ESF-2 also provides communications support to Federal, State, local, and tribal governments and first responders when their systems have been impacted, and provides communications and IT support to the joint field office (JFO) and JFO field teams. With the rapid convergence of communications and IT, NCS and NCSD work closely to coordinate the ESF-2 response to cyber incidents. This convergence requires increased synchronization of efforts and capabilities between the Communications and IT Sectors to facilitate ESF-2's ability to respond to all types of incidents.

---

[9] National Security Telecommunications Advisory Committee Report to the President on Emergency Communications and Interoperability, National Security Telecommunications Advisory Committee, January 16, 2007.

Communications Sector Coordination Groups

In the Communications Sector, partnerships are the foundation for all protective programs. The following are five of the most significant partnerships for infrastructure protection within the sector because they are forums for improving situational awareness, sharing information, developing best practices, and providing policy analysis and recommendations:

The NCS COP is an interagency group designated by the President that provides advice and recommendations on NS/EP communications to the EOP. High-level officials representing Federal operational, policy, regulatory, and enforcement organizations make up the COP. Its diverse representation across the 24 Federal departments and agencies of NCS embraces the full spectrum of Federal telecommunications assets and responsibilities. The COP enables Communications Sector partners across the Federal Government to provide input and guidance to the sector, as well as the EOP, regarding the current status of and future of the sector as a whole.

The NCC serves as a joint industry-government operations center with the mission to coordinate response and restoration priorities during an incident. In addition, through its ISAC function, NCC partners actively share information about threats, vulnerabilities, intrusions, and anomalies.

US-CERT implements the DHS cybersecurity objectives, including how DHS will coordinate and collaborate with public, private, and international partners to help protect and defend the Nation's interests against threats from cyberspace. US-CERT serves as a vital sector partner for the Communications Sector. US-CERT and the NCC embarked on a collocation strategy during the winter of 2008 to help increase information exchange between the IT and Communications Sectors. The two have combined their watch floors to form the NCCIC.

The Government and NSTAC NSIEs meet every two months to share information and views on threats and incidents affecting the public network's software elements and the network's vulnerabilities and possible remedies. In addition, NSIE members periodically assess the risk to the public network (PN) from electronic intrusion. The U.S. NSIE holds multilateral exchange meetings with its counterparts from the United Kingdom, Canada, Australia, and New Zealand.

The ECPC serves as the focal point and clearinghouse for intergovernmental information on interoperable emergency communications and coordinates Federal input to the NECP. To facilitate Federal participation in the NECP process, the ECPC has a focus group comprising representatives from numerous DHS components, as well as DoD, DOJ, the U.S. Department of Commerce (DOC), the U.S. Department of the Treasury, the U.S. Department of the Interior, the FCC, the U.S. National Guard, and others.

Interoperability Programs

The Federal Partnership for Interoperable Communications (FPIC) addresses Federal wireless communications interoperability by fostering intergovernmental cooperation. As a coordinating body, FPIC focuses on technical and operational matters within the Federal wireless communications community, representing more than 40 Federal entities. FPIC has four standing committees that meet monthly to focus on interoperability, security, spectrum, and standards, respectively.

The Statewide Interoperability Coordinators (SWICs) Council comprises the communications interoperability coordinators and SCIP POCs from each of the 50 States and six Territories. OEC supports SWICs in the implementation of their SCIP and equips SWICs with tools, best practices, and policy information. Additionally, OEC engages SWICs to gain input on OEC policies and programs. SWICs meet twice a year in person.

The SAFECOM Executive Committee (EC) and Emergency Response Council (ERC) comprise State, local, and tribal emergency response officials and association representatives, and provide input to OEC and OIC on emergency communications policies, programs, and initiatives. OEC engages the EC and ERC regularly, with monthly, quarterly, and biannual meetings.

Industry Protective Measures and Initiatives

Industry efforts to protect their assets include, but are not limited to, multi-billion dollar investments to improve redundancy and resilience by adding generators, improving physical security at facilities, improving crisis management processes and protocols, and performing audits to increase the level of protection. Communications Sector companies plan to continue to improve industry and government threat and vulnerability information sharing, including vital information related to cyber-security. The CSCC views information sharing as a fundamental element of effective preparedness and response actions. The effects of disruptive activity associated with virtually all incidents of a manmade or natural nature can be mitigated if timely and actionable information is provided.

Industry participates in a variety of venues that are designed to promote this type of two-way information sharing. This involves industry representation in the current NCC environment and future engagement in the merged NCCIC. Furthermore, industry participation in numerous standards development organizations (e.g., the Alliance for Telecommunications Industry Solutions and the International Organization for Standardization) and public emergency organizations (e.g., NENA), and engagement with State organizations (e.g., NARUC) support and enhance an environment in which information regarding CIKR, situational awareness and operational plans are openly discussed, reviewed, and enhanced.

Through the CSCC and other partnership entities, industry will continue to develop and participate in threat simulations and exercises, including those that test cybersecurity readiness and response capabilities. Industry's primary goals in exercise participation are to identify operational constraints and to improve overall response performance. Industry observations regarding the planning and execution of recent National Level Exercises (NLEs) revealed the need for greater industry participation early in the planning process to ensure that exercises realistically reflect on-the-ground realities and that the impact on Communications Sector assets and functions is appropriately factored into exercise scenarios. In 2010, the CSCC, C-ISAC, and their member companies and associations are collaborating with government entities to plan and execute Cyber Storm III, which will center on cyber-focused scenarios that will escalate to a level requiring a coordinated national and international response, involving companies and government organizations in the United States, United Kingdom, Canada, Australia, and New Zealand.

Industry plans to continue to develop POC networks in regional, State, and local environments to facilitate more effective coordination in cases where disruptions may impact physical and cyber assets and functions. Current efforts are underway on a POC initiative sponsored by NARUC. Other contact efforts are occurring between the CSCC and MS-ISAC in the area of cyber situational awareness. Additional regional outreach involves coordination with FEMA regional offices, NCS regional representatives, and State fusion centers.

Industry will also continue to educate stakeholders on communications infrastructure resilience and risk management practices, including cybersecurity. The CSCC Outreach Committee coordinates these educational efforts, which include routine presentations to congressional and Federal Government departmental stakeholders, as well as other SCCs and industry leaders. In addition, individual companies will continue to engage in numerous presentations and discussions with State stakeholders, including regulators, on the capabilities that they offer for resilience and risk mitigation decisions. Ongoing effective cross-sector coordination mechanisms with a cybersecurity emphasis include PCIS, CSCSWG, the ISAC Council, and NCS.

Physical Security: These measures will vary depending on the characteristics of the asset's location, the function in the architecture, and customer requirements. Types of assets typically include data centers, switch sites, point of presence (POP) sites, warehouses, call centers, retail stores, and general office buildings. For example, transmission lines that are omnipresent cannot receive the same level of security as an end office or a teleport. Similarly, an end office in a rural area will likely not have the same security level as one in an urban area. Furthermore, physical security assessments are conducted based on the criticality of the asset to verify compliance with policies, standards, contracts, and regulations (see the Industry Self-Assessments subsection in chapter 3).

Cyber/Logical Security: The Nation's communications infrastructure is inextricably linked to cyber infrastructure. All sector assets, systems, and networks include cyber infrastructure people, process, and technology elements that enable the efficient and effective functioning of information and computer systems and generation, transmission, and delivery of data, voice, and video over fixed and mobile assets. Table 5-1 illustrates cybersecurity-focused programs and initiatives within the Communications Sector.

Table 5-1: Communications Sector Cybersecurity Infrastructure Components

People Components	
National Cybersecurity and Communications Integration Center (NCCIC)	The NCCIC relies on cyber infrastructure people elements by promoting the collocation of industry and governmental operations center personnel. The NCCIC improves the Nation's capability and capacity to detect, prevent, respond to, and mitigate disruptions of voice and cyber communications by unifying vital IT and communications operations centers, starting with the NCC and US-CERT. The NCC serves as a joint industry-government operations center with a mission to coordinate response and restoration priorities during an incident. In addition, through its ISAC function, NCC partners actively share information about threats, vulnerabilities, intrusions, and anomalies. US-CERT implements the DHS cybersecurity objectives, including how DHS will coordinate and collaborate with public, private, and international partners to help protect and defend the Nation's interests against threats from cyberspace. US-CERT serves as a vital sector partner for the Communications Sector.
Network Security Information Exchanges (NSIEs)	NSIEs rely on cyber infrastructure people elements by facilitating meetings every two months to share information and views on threats and incidents affecting the public network's software elements and the network's vulnerabilities and possible remedies. In addition, NSIE members periodically assess the risk to the PN from electronic intrusion. The U.S. NSIEs hold multilateral exchange meetings with counterparts from the United Kingdom, Canada, Australia, and New Zealand.
Process Components	
Emergency Support Function 2 (ESF-2)	ESF-2 relies on cyber infrastructure processes by supporting the restoration of the communications infrastructure, facilitating the recovery of systems and applications from cyber attacks, and coordinating Federal communications support to response efforts during incidents that require a coordinated Federal response. This ESF implements the provisions of the OSTP NPTS.
Cyber Storm III	The Cyber Storm exercise series is a cyber infrastructure process element. Cyber Storm enables industry and government partners to exercise the plans, capabilities, and procedures necessary to ensure the security of the Nation's broad and interdependent cyber infrastructure. Members of the Communications Sector have participated in the initial two Cyber Storm exercises and will be participating in Cyber Storm III in 2010 to: • Identify and exercise the processes, procedures, relationships, and mechanisms for effectively addressing a cyber event/threat; • Examine DHS's role in a global cyber event; • Focus on information-sharing issues during cyber events; and • Examine coordination and decisionmaking procedures/mechanisms across government and with the private sector and international partners.

Process Components (continued)	
Partnership for Critical Infrastructure Security (PCIS)	PCIS relies on cyber infrastructure process elements and focuses on cross-sector policy, strategy, and interdependency issues, including cybersecurity, which affect the critical infrastructure sectors. PCIS members include the leadership from each of the SCCs, representing the owners and operators of the 18 CIKR sectors identified by the NIPP.
Cross-Sector Cyber Security Working Group (CSCSWG)	CSCSWG is a process element of the cyber infrastructure and was established to improve cross-sector cybersecurity protection efforts across the Nation's CIKR sectors by: • Identifying opportunities to improve sector coordination on cybersecurity issues and topics; • Highlighting cyber dependencies and interdependencies; and • Sharing government and private sector cybersecurity products and findings. The working group serves as a forum in which public and private sector partners share perspectives, knowledge, and subject matter expertise on a wide range of cybersecurity issues. CSCSWG aligns with the NIPP sector partnership model, including members from the SCCs and GCCs of the 18 CIKR sectors.
Technology Components	
Government Emergency Telecommunications Service (GETS)	GETS relies on cyber technology elements, including routers, switches, protocols, and other specialized hardware and software, to provide emergency access and priority processing in the local and long-distance segments of the PSTN. This service increases the likelihood that NS/EP personnel can complete critical calls during periods of PSTN disruption and congestion resulting from natural or manmade disasters. GETS uses three major types of networks: major long-distance networks, local networks, and government-leased networks.
Wireless Priority Service (WPS)	WPS relies on cyber technology elements, including protocols and specialized hardware and software, to provide priority commercial mobile radio service during and after emergencies for NS/EP personnel. WPS ensures that NS/EP calls receive the next available radio channel during times of wireless congestion.

Human Security and the Insider Threat

Approaches to human security and insider threats vary depending on a company's human resources policies. Companies may screen employees to confirm their backgrounds and ensure the necessary trustworthiness; rotate assignments to reduce the chance of fraud and misuse of resources; enforce separation of duties and least-privilege policies; conduct periodic security awareness training; implement password and account management policies and practices; log, monitor, and audit employee online activity; monitor and respond to suspicious or disruptive behavior; and deactivate access following employee termination. The purpose of these procedures is to mitigate the threat posed by insiders and a company's reliance on individual employees. The Communications Sector also uses robust business continuity plans that assess threats, vulnerabilities, and countermeasures and sound business practices that develop and maintain an appropriate state of resilience and preparedness within the company.

Outreach

The CSCC's Outreach Committee will help ensure that the SCC is prepared to educate policymakers on the work that Communications Sector private sector partners are performing regarding CIKR protection. The industry will also continue to educate sector partners on communications infrastructure resilience and risk management practices. Several outreach efforts have been conducted at the Federal and State levels, including congressional meetings. Going forward, the Outreach Committee will continue to educate sector partners on communications infrastructure resilience and risk management practices in the Communications Sector. The CSCC will work to establish measures that will reflect progress in this area.

Industry partners regularly work with enterprise customers to educate them on risks and mitigation strategies. In addition to joint outreach activities conducted through the coordinating council framework, Communications Sector partners will continue to conduct customer outreach. These outreach activities will educate customers about the CSSP and the risk variables that customers need to consider as part of their own business continuity practices, as well as resilience best practices. The Communications Sector will collaborate with the IT Sector on outreach to and education of customers about their reliance on communications and IT infrastructure and the corresponding security roles and responsibilities. Future outreach will also include educating customers about the results of risk assessments to help prioritize the implementation of mitigation measures that are relevant to the customer.

The CSCC continues to support efforts that enable safe and efficient access to disaster recovery sites by essential service providers, as well as support and coordination for credentialing and perimeter access protocols (for essential service providers) across Federal, regional, State, and local jurisdictions. This is especially important given that perimeter access policies, in general, are governed by State and local regulation and enforcement.[10]

Private sector partners develop POCs in State government to facilitate regional coordination and participate in State and local emergency operations centers and facilitated regional coordination efforts.

As addressed in previous chapters, customers also have a responsibility for protecting the communications infrastructure. Corporate customers should assist in mitigating risk by developing communications backup plans and implementing resilience measures (e.g., geographic diversity). Infrastructure owners and operators do not always know how, when, and where their customers are using their assets and what critical business functions they may be running on those communications assets. Communications Sector industry partners engage customers on their responsibilities and provide information on the preparedness and protective actions that customers can take to mitigate risks.

Protecting Assets

Companies have dedicated departments with responsibility for their physical assets, and these departments direct coordinated efforts that lead to the detection, apprehension, and, when deemed advisable, the prosecution of individuals who perpetrate or attempt to perpetrate criminal acts against a company's assets. These internal groups serve as the primary liaison with law enforcement and internal coordination for the reporting of criminal acts against their company. Through partnerships with internal business units and external law enforcement, the communications industry conducts factual, detailed, and thorough investigations. Departments continue to ensure timely, relevant, and accurate threat information sharing among law enforcement, intelligence communities, and key decisionmakers in the sector. Owners and operators have developed protocols for engagement with State fusion centers. The CSCC has established measures to reflect progress in this area.

Cyber Elements of the Sector's Protection Plan

Similar to the other security elements, cyber elements will vary across the sector; however, some common practices exist. For example, two common practices that carriers follow to ensure the security of signaling and control planes are (1) Access Control Lists (ACL) that filter IP packets destined to the router in specific IP address and protocol ranges to protect the router management plane and router control plane, and (2) Reverse Path Forwarding that checks the source IP address to protect against spoofing and denial-of-service attacks and drops packets when the source address does not match the packet's origin path.

The Communications Sector was heavily involved in the Conficker Working Group to develop mitigation techniques to respond to the evolving threat. The industry will continue to identify programs to deter, respond to, and recover from cyber attacks, as well as keep government partners informed as cyber events unfold.

---

[10] 2009 Communications Sector Annual Report, section 5.3.2.3.

Table 5-2: Examples of Protective Measure

	Protective Category	Protective Measure Examples
Protection	Deter	Facility surveillance Facility and network access controls
	Devalue	Backup network operations centers Synchronous optical network ring networks
	Detect	Facility alarm systems Network monitoring
	Defend	Buffer zones for critical facilities Firewalls on control system networks
Preparedness	Mitigate	Self-healing networks Redundant signaling systems GETS, WPS, NCC
	Respond	Emergency response plans, procedures, and exercises
	Recover	Business continuity plans Mutual-aid agreements NCC, TSP

5.2 Determining the Need for Protective Programs and Resilience Strategies

NCS works through the NCC and its partners to conduct incident and event response analysis. This analysis of the telecommunications infrastructure helps NCS determine telecommunications impacts that result from various classes of events.

Regional Characterizations

The sector conducted regional characterizations to provide an assessment of nationwide critical communications assets and networks to assess and identify high-risk areas prior to an emergency. Each characterization provides an analysis of a significant regional communications agency and site, and the results of each characterization are incorporated into NCS analytical tools and models to support other assessments.

Cross-Sector Analysis

Cross-sector dependency analyses reflect the results of both qualitative and analytical risk analyses that consider threats, vulnerabilities, and consequences. As such, these assessments determine the magnitude and duration of the effects based on reliable threat data using both risk and sector experts. Based on research, sector experts will determine the key sectors that the Communications Sector depends on to remain operational. Each analysis demonstrates the Communications Sector's dependence on other sectors, assists other sectors in the assessment of communications dependencies for high-risk infrastructure, and identifies high-risk items from other sectors—such as Transportation Systems (e.g., train stations) and Commercial Facilities (e.g., the Empire State Building)—for collateral damage considerations to the Communications Sector.

Exercises

The Communications Sector participates in exercises that test and evaluate its analytical capabilities in response to various scenarios. In preparation for the 2008 hurricane season, the ESF-2 exercises assessed the capabilities of Federal, State, and local governments and private industry in responding to catastrophic events. DHS sponsored Eagle Horizon 2008, which was an exercise partnership of NCS, the General Services Administration, the FCC, the National Telecommunications and Information Administration (NTIA), FEMA, and the U.S. Department of Agriculture (USDA). Because continuity of communications is critical to COG and COOP, upcoming exercises will attempt to create emergency and disaster recovery scenarios in which communications are severely degraded or present an outage condition. Close coordination and cooperation between government and the communications industry will be required in planning and executing realistic communications situations, their remediation, and/or restoration as part of upcoming exercises. A detailed list of these exercises is available in appendix F.

5.3 Protective Programs and Resilience Strategy Implementation

Coordination and Implementation of Protective Programs

In recognition of the shared protective responsibilities between industry and government, the Communications Sector coordinates the development of protective measure strategies as part of the risk analysis process and the prioritization of risk assessment results. Based on the prioritization of risks, the SSA, the CGCC, and the CSCC meets to determine whether a new government protective program is necessary. This determination rests on the following factors:

• Impact on the entire communications infrastructure;

• Imminence of the threat;

• Magnitude of the vulnerability;

• Cost-benefit analysis;

• Available funding; and

• Effectiveness of existing or potential protective measures in reducing risk.

In the event that a new government protective program is necessary, appropriate partners (e.g., the CSCC, the CGCC, and the IT Sector) will be identified and roles and responsibilities for developing agreed-upon protective measures will be assigned. Partners may include select owners and operators, equipment manufacturers, trade associations, and appropriate government agencies for programs focused on the communications infrastructure. For programs geared toward addressing dependencies with other critical infrastructure, NCS will engage the appropriate SSAs.

The protective program development and implementation process builds on the sector goals and their affiliated and prioritized high-risk infrastructure, as determined by the processes described in previous chapters. Government-sponsored protective programs enable industry to work together to address issues that it normally would not address collectively due to competitive reasons.

The protective program development and implementation process will ensure that government protective programs are logically linked to specific goals and critical risks to justify the cost. Industry is encouraged to undertake similar processes to justify its protective programs.

Validation of Protective Programs

To help guide and validate protective programs, NCS also will continue to consult two of its trusted partners—the NCS COP and NSTAC—to identify shortfalls and weaknesses in the NS/EP communications infrastructure and to recommend appropriate action. Through the COP process, NCS provides NS/EP communications recommendations to the EOP. NSTAC provides crucial advice and recommendations to the President and the Secretary of Homeland Security on the development and conduct of NS/EP communications programs.

Funding is a major issue that affects all security and protective initiatives, including those within the communications industry. Implementation of recommended or agreed upon sector protective measures will depend on the availability of resources combined with a determination of which costs should be borne by the Federal Government or State and local entities versus costs which should be borne by industry.

5.4 Monitoring Protective Programs and Resilience Strategy Implementation

New protection priorities identified through the risk assessment process may require additional protective programs. These protective programs are likely to fall into three categories: (1) private sector initiatives, (2) Federal Government programs, and (3) State government projects.

- **Private Sector Initiatives:** These initiatives typically require a business case for justification. They may be developed by owners and operators to voluntarily respond to specific vulnerabilities identified during risk assessments, and may be in the form of voluntary best practices, standards, or individual company protective measures. Individual owners and operators or trade associations will develop, implement, and maintain these initiatives.

- **Federal Government Programs:** NS/EP institutions will be monitored to ensure compliance with current Federal directives that mandate telecommunications continuity as part of every NS/EP institution's COOP and COG plan. A relationship will be maintained with relevant service providers and operators, and with equipment manufacturers throughout the process.

- **State Government Projects:** These projects allow State agencies to coordinate with one another and with their Federal and private sector counterparts. NARUC and the States have begun to work with the FCC and others to develop emergency POC networks in PUCs, emergency management agencies, Governors' offices, and elsewhere to facilitate regional coordination and to mitigate the effects on interdependent sectors, when appropriate.

NCS will discuss successes and lessons learned from protective program performance in the Sector CIKR Protection Annual Report (hereinafter referred to as the Sector Annual Report). The annual report will be shared with sector partners.

Additionally, Title XVIII of the Homeland Security Act charges OEC's Director with conducting periodic assessments of the state of interoperability. The OEC Director is also responsible for regularly reporting to Congress on progress toward achieving national objectives and the effectiveness of methods to address emerging emergency communications vulnerabilities.

6. Measure Effectiveness

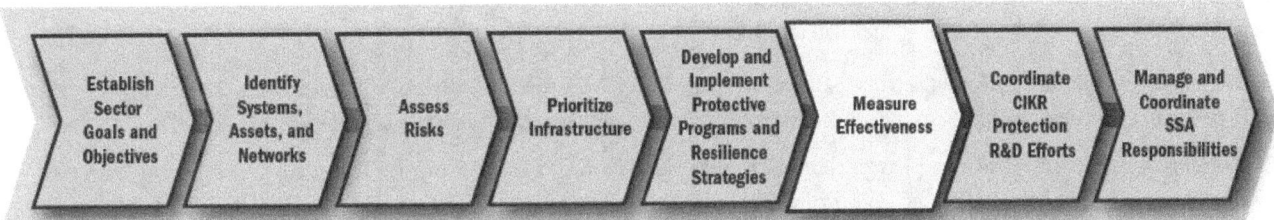

The Communications Sector measures its collective success based on progress achieved toward CSSP goals. These goals continue to evolve over time according to changes in the sector's risk and business environments. The Communications Sector's framework identifies, monitors, and evaluates its successes in sector-wide risk management efforts.

This chapter reviews the framework and the specific measures used by the Communications Sector. The measures are reviewed annually and in the aftermath of major events. Performance results allow the sector to make more informed decisions on protective investments and process improvements.

6.1 Risk Mitigation Activities

As defined by the NIPP, a risk mitigation activity (RMA) is a program, tool, or initiative that directly or indirectly reduces risk in the sector, including providing for the sector's resilience. The Communications Sector completed specific actions and milestones identified in the 2009 Sector Annual Report and aligned existing CIKR protective programs and risk management activities with the goals highlighted earlier within this plan. Appendix F describes the key RMAs identified by the Communications Sector that have the highest potential impact on the sector's security and/or make the greatest contribution toward mitigating the risk to the sector's CIKR infrastructure. Each key RMA equally contributes to the overall security of the sector and specifically addresses the goals and objectives set forth by the sector. The RMAs are reported to the NIPP through the Sector Annual Report and serve as a prime example of how the sector measures its effectiveness in CIKR protection.

6.2 Process for Measuring Effectiveness

The performance measurement process requires close collaboration in monitoring sector progress in critical infrastructure protection, response and recovery, awareness, and cross-sector coordination.

Performance measures promote Communications Sector awareness of the status of sector risk mitigation activities and the progress of related programs and activities using specific progress indicators to reflect the milestones achieved. Sector metrics measure the sector's success in meeting its goals and provide quantifiable snapshots of performance trends over time. Trend analysis will facilitate the benchmarking of sector success in meeting goals and cataloging the impact of sector progress.

With respect to measuring effectiveness, Communications Sector partners work together to accomplish the following:

- Collect responses to metrics from the sector;
- Ensure the accuracy of the information collected;
- Report metrics to DHS; and
- Ensure that metrics meet the needs of DHS with regard to monitoring performance across the Communications Sector.

Process for Measuring Sector Progress

Metrics are tools that are designed to facilitate decisionmaking, performance improvement, and accountability through the collection, analysis, and reporting of relevant performance data. To ensure that metrics are useful for tracking performance and facilitating performance improvement, the metrics must:

- **Be Based on Performance Goals:** Sector goals for industry and government partners are identified and prioritized to ensure that performance measures correspond with the operational priorities of the Communications Sector.

- **Yield Quantifiable Information:** Metrics should produce the data necessary for making comparisons, applying formulas, and tracking changes using the same points of reference. When quantifiable information is unavailable, meaningful qualitative indicators will be substituted.

- **Be Obtainable and Repeatable:** Data for calculating metrics need to be easily obtainable and repeatable (i.e., obtainable on a regular basis) to enable analysis of performance trends over time.

To adhere to these fundamental aspects of sound performance measurement, the Communications Sector uses the Performance Measurement Framework depicted in figure 6-1 to develop its sector-specific metrics. As figure 6-1 illustrates, feedback loops are built into the performance measurement framework. As the Communications Sector continues to mature, feedback loops will ensure that goals, policies, and procedures are updated, as necessary. Steps 1 through 3 include identifying sector-specific partners, as well as applicable goals and policies that govern the sector. Steps 4 through 7 measure the sector's progress toward achieving goals and compliance with applicable policies and procedures through a maturing series of measurement indicators. Feedback mechanisms will be used to update and amend the measurement framework over time.

Figure 6-1: Communications Sector Performance Measurement Framework

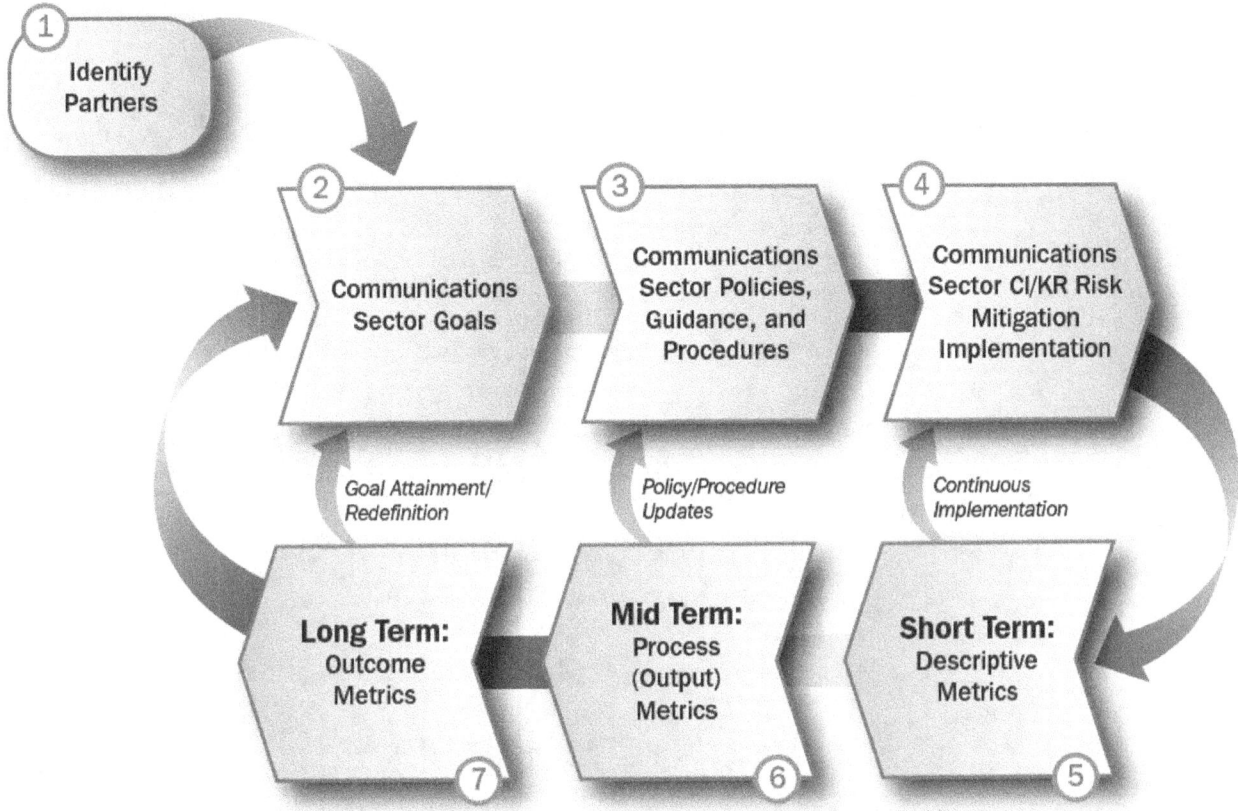

Step 1 of the Communications Sector Performance Measurement Framework involves identifying Communications Sector partners. The number and mix of Communications Sector industry and government partners in this process will evolve over time.

Step 2 involves identifying Communications Sector goals that will guide performance by industry and government partners. These goals serve as performance objectives and will frame the measurement process. These goals are defined in chapter 1.

Step 3 involves examining applicable sector-specific policies and procedures for securing and ensuring the resilience of Communications Sector infrastructure. These policies and procedures describe the key activities and responsibilities of industry and government partners in the Communications Sector. Specific sector policies, authorities, directives, and orders are explained in detail in appendix C. These high-level policies will be combined with sector goals to establish the measurement process for industry and government partners within the Communications Sector.

Step 4 involves establishing measures to assess the sector's performance against its goals, policies, and procedures from Steps 2 and 3. Performance measures will help determine the effectiveness of risk mitigation efforts and whether specific activities and programs need to be continued, modified, or cancelled to best meet sector goals. Specific metrics will be mapped to sector goals to provide a robust assessment of sector performance.

As part of Step 4, metrics will be designed to support and demonstrate progress toward Communications Sector goals. Table 6-1 illustrates the sector goals and the potential areas of measurement for each goal. The measurement areas will be used to help create and approve relevant metrics. Industry and government partners will be involved in the metric creation and approval process. NCS, together with Communications Sector Measurement Working Group participants, will develop metrics based on the measurement areas for each goal. Each metric will be documented in a standard template to help ensure consistency. Table 6-2 illustrates the metric template.[11]

Table 6-1: Potential Communications Sector Measurement Areas

Goals	Activity
Goal 1: Protect and enhance the overall physical and logical health of communications.	Implement security processes and best practices to: • Protect the backbone; • Standardize the screening process for relevant personnel with access to communications assets; • Access control best practices and insider threat mitigation best practices; and • Promote industry and government threat and vulnerability information sharing.
Goal 2: Rapidly reconstitute critical communications services in the event of disruption and mitigate cascading effects.	Implement processes and procedures in order to rapidly respond to crises that affect the communications infrastructure and promote COOP during crises
Goal 3: Improve the sector's national security and emergency preparedness (NS/EP) posture with Federal, State, local, tribal, international, and private sector entities to reduce risk.	Develop and participate in threat simulations and exercises; Develop educational programs on communications technologies and their potential points of failure during emergencies; Participate in conferences, trade shows, and outreach activities related to priority service programs; Develop and participate in cross-sector threat exercises; and Develop and participate in cross-sector working groups.

[11] The metrics template aligns with the metrics template found in National Institute of Standards and Technology (NIST) Special Publication 800-55, Security Metrics Guide for Information Technology Systems, October 2002.

Table 6-2: Communications Sector Metrics Template

Metric Component	Description
Performance Goal	Communications Sector goal that the metric supports
Purpose	Intended to obtain overall functionality by collecting the metric, what insights are hoped to be gained from the metric, regulatory or legal reasons for collecting a specific metric if such exist, and other similar items
Implementation Evidence	Used to calculate the metric, provides indirect indicators that validate that the activity has been performed, identifies causation factors that may point to the causes of unsatisfactory results for a specific metric
Frequency	Time periods for data collection
Formula	Calculation to be performed that results in a numeric expression of a metric
Data Source	Location of the data to be used in calculating the metric and the parties responsible for reporting the data
Indicators	Information about the meaning of the metric and its performance trend; possible causes of trends; possible solutions for correcting the observed shortcomings; performance target, if it has been set for the metric; indication of what trends would be considered positive in relationship to the performance target

As the final part of Step 4, metrics are shared with sector partners for review and comment. Feedback is incorporated into the metric template, and the metrics become official and are tracked for data analysis and reporting purposes according to their frequency, as indicated in the metric template. As Steps 5 through 7 of the Performance Measurement Framework indicate, various metrics yield different results and provide different indicators for Communications Sector industry and government partners.

Step 5 begins the metric data collection process for the sector. It features short-term descriptive measures to assess the implementation of planned sector activities and programs and their subsequent requirements. The descriptive metrics are used to understand sector resources and activities; they do not reflect CIKR protection performance. The Communications Sector Measurement Working Group will develop and advance descriptive measures with Communications Sector partners.

Step 6 shifts from a descriptive metrics focus to an output metrics focus. Output measures help partners determine whether specific activities are proceeding as planned by tracking the progression of a task, reporting on the output of a process such as inventorying assets, or showing progress toward performing the activities necessary to achieve Communications Sector goals.

Step 7 moves from an output metrics focus to an outcome metrics focus. Outcome metrics track progress toward the sector's strategic goals by evaluating beneficial results instead of implementation or activity levels. This, in turn, indicates progress toward reaching sector-specific goals.

As figure 6-1 above illustrates, feedback loops are built into the performance measurement framework. As the Communications Sector continues to mature, feedback loops will ensure that goals, policies, and procedures are updated, as necessary.

Information Collection and Verification

Consistent data collection, verification, analysis, and reporting are crucial to a successful performance measurement effort. The Communications Sector will rely on a metrics information collection and verification strategy determined by sector partners.

Each metric has specific data sources, parties responsible for reporting metric data, and metric reporting frequencies. Because each metric will have different data sources and responsible parties, the NCS GIP&M Branch will be used as a centralized conduit for NCS and its industry and government partners for reporting metric data.

The NCC, in conjunction with its industry and government partners, will employ an online or automated tool with an easy-to-use front end for partners to report data and a data repository back end to store and validate data fields for analysis and reporting purposes. The NCS GIP&M Branch can then transfer the appropriate information to the NIPP online metrics portal.

Reporting

The primary means of Communications Sector reporting will be the Sector Annual Report. This report is submitted to DHS and describes sector goals, priorities, programs, and related funding requirements, as well as a catalogue of progress that has been made in sector CIKR protection. By collecting and reporting metrics results, the Communications Sector will be able to establish a performance baseline and then show progress against the baseline in the ensuing years. In addition, metrics performance data for each goal will allow industry and government partners to identify underperforming areas for the sector quickly and prioritize funding, resources, and activities accordingly to improve sector performance.

The NCS GIP&M Branch will serve as a clearinghouse for sector metrics reporting from industry and government partners. The NCS GIP&M Branch will collect sector-reported information, report it to the NIPP online metrics portal, and aggregate data for the Sector Annual Report. Further information on reporting is detailed in chapter 8.

Aligning Outcome-Based Metrics to Protective Programs

Once government programs have been developed and implemented, NCS will conduct follow-up risk assessments on government protective programs to measure their success in reducing overall risk after about two years of full implementation. When a program overlaps the Communications and IT Sectors, there will be a joint program review. This evaluation process will include the following steps:

- Program briefing with the program manager;
- Follow-up interviews with program users (if relevant);
- Site assessment (if relevant);
- Update to the risk assessment of relevant architecture element(s);
- Cost-benefit analysis; and
- Program performance evaluation.

The performance evaluation will assess the program's effectiveness and make recommendations for potential changes or enhancements. With the high rate of technological advances in the Communications Sector, these performance evaluations will need to consider changes in technology, which may lead to enhancements in some programs, while discontinuing other programs that are no longer relevant.

6.3 Using Metrics for Continuous Improvement

As demonstrated in figure 6-1, the Communications Sector will use a time-phased approach to performance measurement, using descriptive, process, and outcome measures as sector measurement activities mature to examine sector performance in mitigating CIKR risk. Throughout the measurement process, feedback mechanisms will help update and amend the framework, as needed, to accommodate sector changes and maturity. Feedback with regard to the initial descriptive measures and sector protection initiatives and programs will help guide protection implementation activities. Process metrics will help reexamine sector policies and procedures. Outcome measures will measure sector goal attainment.

The measurement process is an important part of the overall risk management framework because it gauges industry and government partner progress and gaps in meeting sector goals and, in turn, informs protective program improvements and changes to risk management processes. When gaps are identified, NCS will review them with industry and government partners to determine useful corrective actions. Outcomes could include revising sector goals to account for changes in the threat environment, addressing protective programs, and calling for a new R&D initiative. As detailed in chapter 8, the NCS GIP&M Branch will work with the NCS Plans and Resources Branch to track and manage the aspects of the NCS budget that are related to infrastructure protection. The performance measurement process will be used to prioritize resource requests to ensure that the budget is aligned toward effective programs.

7. Coordinate CIKR Protection R&D Efforts

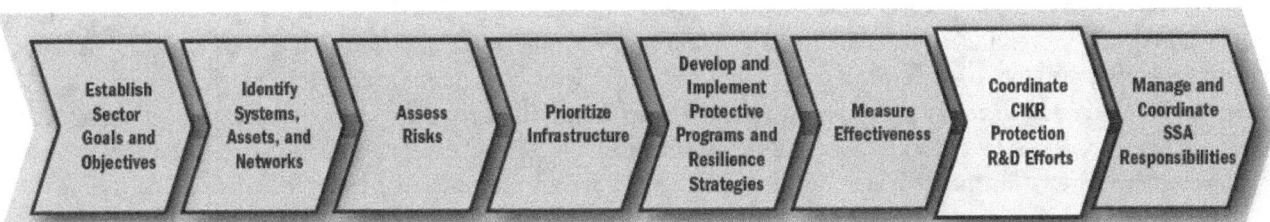

The modern communications infrastructure—made possible by research performed over the last several decades—is an essential element of the U.S. economy and society. Communications research has yielded major direct benefits such as the Internet, radio frequency wireless communications, broadband, optical networks, and Voice Over IP (VoIP). Communications has expanded greatly from analog broadcasting and primarily landline telephone service to fully digital broadcasting (television) and the use of fiber-optic, cable, satellite, and wireless connections offering a wide range of voice, image, video, and data services. Many of the new challenges facing the Communications Sector call for innovations in science and technology, making R&D initiatives essential to sector CIKR protection. Furthermore, one of HSPD-7's requirements is the development of an R&D plan for CIKR protection. This chapter addresses the R&D planning processes (summarized in figure 7-1) for the Communications Sector, which calls for not only hard science but also people-oriented R&D.

Figure 7-1: The R&D Process

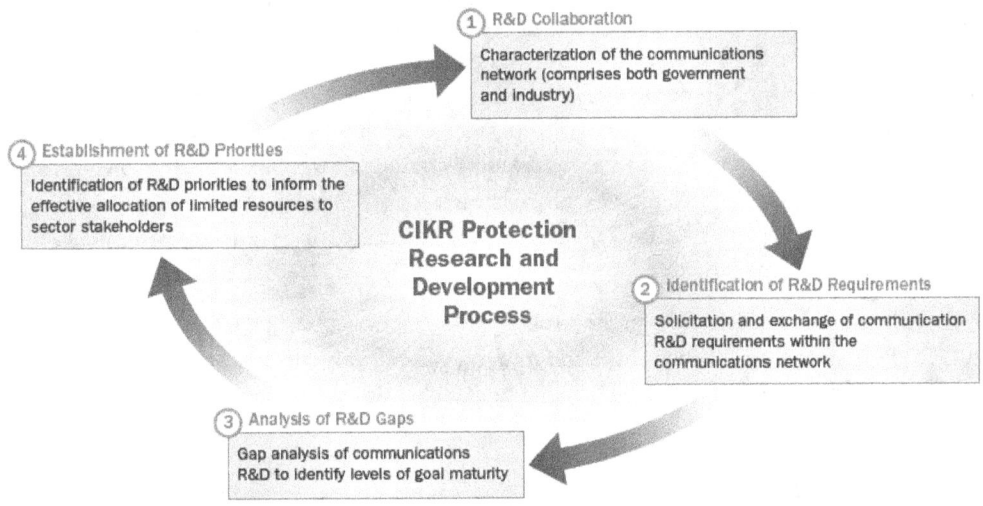

7.1 Overview of Sector Research and Development

The United States has a critical reliance on ensured communications; the Communications Sector's R&D agenda is focused on efforts to ensure that communications networks and systems are available, secure, resilient, and rapidly restored in the event of disruption. The Federal Government's obligation to protect the American people and to provide for the common defense includes responsibility for ensuring the ability to communicate and respond in times of crisis.

The diverse array of players within the Communications Sector, from the multiple government R&D initiatives to the competing communications firms—telephone, cable, Internet, and wireless—makes it more challenging to design and deploy the major, end-to-end innovations that are necessary to support sector goals. Multiple visions are now being pursued by various segments of the communications industry, which makes widespread deployment of technology that improves CIKR protection more complex. The reality is that no single entity can comprehensively address the engineering and standardization issues associated with the end-to-end solutions that must span multiple service providers and multiple sectors of the industry.

These CIKR protection challenges cannot be addressed through traditional forms of R&D sponsored by government agencies, private industry, and universities. Issues include both physical and electronic information security, as well as new threats and vulnerabilities from the growing and complex interdependence among the critical infrastructure. These challenges might be addressed with the assistance of a public-private R&D roadmap to streamline research priorities across the sector. Such a framework would provide a fresh examination of R&D requirements and identify gaps in technology development. To succeed, an unprecedented partnership that combines the best resources of government, academia, and private industry needs to be undertaken to tackle these new challenges.

Continuing R&D efforts within the sector include:

- Next generation of alert and warning systems;
- Next generation of priority services;
- New digital technology for interoperability; and
- Identity management solutions.

Industry Coordination

Success and failure in today's communications marketplace hinges on an organization's ability to transform ideas, problems, or needs into improved products and processes or new businesses and revenues. Successful innovation in the current economic climate requires new tools, practices, and collaborative partnerships. Quickly getting products to market has always been a major concern. More and more successful R&D organizations are leveraging their technologies across internal and external partnerships and are creating networks of strategic alliances and cross-industry collaborations. Every year since 1993, the Industrial Research Institute's (IRI) R&D Trends Forecast has asked member companies to identify the biggest problem that they face as R&D leaders.[12] Every year since 2002, IRI member companies have reported that "growing the business through innovation" is their biggest problem; other top problem areas include accelerating innovation, balancing long-term and short-term R&D objectives, and integrating technology planning with business strategy. Encouraging and managing innovation is a key business process that enhances a company's future. This has become especially true within the communications industry due to the changes in the market and industry structure.

The government depends on private companies, in their role as owners, operators, integrators, suppliers and innovators, to share responsibility for increasing the resilience of the communications infrastructure. Government coordination is needed to provide a methodology for developing important end-to-end capabilities. Communications and IT R&D advances the digital

---

[12] Cosner, Raymond R., R&D Trends Forecast for 2009, Research Technology Management, The Industrial Research Institute, January 2009.

technologies that power critical NS/EP capabilities. A strong, collaborative R&D program advances the resilience of telecommunications and information systems.

NSTAC examines areas for future development and seeks to enhance coordination between the public and private sectors and the academic research community. Periodically, the NSTAC Industry Executive Subcommittee Research and Development Task Force (RDTF) conducts an R&D Exchange (RDX) Workshop to stimulate and facilitate dialogue among industry, government, and academia on emerging security technology R&D activities that impact CIKR protection. To ensure the inclusion of all stakeholders in the R&D community, the RDTF traditionally invites representatives from a broad number of private sector companies, academic institutions, and key government agencies with NS/EP and/or R&D responsibilities such as OSTP, the Defense Advanced Research Projects Agency (DARPA), the DHS S&T Directorate, and the National Institute of Standards and Technology (NIST). Over the course of the workshop, participants endeavor to frame key policy issues, identify and characterize barriers and impediments inhibiting R&D, discuss how stakeholders can cooperate and coordinate efforts as the communities of interest shift, and develop specific and realistic recommendations for further action by key stakeholders and decisionmakers. The results of the RDX Workshop are published in a proceedings document, which provides important input into the Federal Government's research agenda for NS/EP communications.

The sector also coordinates overlapping critical infrastructure protection R&D priorities with established mechanisms under the NIPP as Federal departments and agencies work with State and local governments and the private sector to identify, prioritize, and coordinate the protection of critical infrastructure. DHS established CIPAC to facilitate effective coordination between Federal infrastructure protection programs and the infrastructure protection activities of the private sector and State, local, tribal, and territorial governments. CIPAC represents a partnership between government and CIKR owners and operators and provides a forum in which they can engage in a broad spectrum of activities to support and coordinate critical infrastructure protection. Also, the CIKR Cross-Sector Council coordinates cross-sector initiatives that promote public and private efforts to help ensure secure, safe, and reliable critical infrastructure services, working through PCIS. This mission encompasses physical, cyber, and human security that rely on strong infrastructure integrity and resilience.

Interagency Coordination

In February 2009, President Barack Obama directed the National Security Council and the Homeland Security Council to conduct a 60-day review of the plans, programs, and activities underway throughout government that address our communications and information infrastructure in order to develop a strategic framework to ensure that the U.S. Government's initiatives in this area are appropriately integrated, resourced, and coordinated.[13] Threats to the communications and information infrastructure pose one of the most serious economic and national security challenges of the 21st century. Because vital U.S. interests (e.g., national defense communications, financial markets, and the operation of critical infrastructure such as power grids) now depend on secure, reliable, high-speed network connectivity, vulnerabilities can threaten our national security and economic competitiveness. R&D to create and secure the next generation of networking technologies is needed to address these threats. Broad areas of concern include network security; the confidentiality, availability, and integrity of information and systems; new approaches to achieving hardware and software security; testing and assessment of systems security; and reconstitution and recovery of systems and data.

The Networking and Information Technology Research and Development (NITRD) Program is the Nation's primary source of Federal funding for advanced technologies such as computing, networking, and software. The NITRD program is a unique collaboration of more than a dozen Federal R&D agencies, including the National Science Foundation (NSF), DARPA, and DoD research organizations, the National Security Agency, NIST, the National Aeronautics and Space Administration (NASA), and DHS, among others. The NITRD program seeks to accelerate deployment of advanced and experimental technologies to

---

[13] White House Cyberspace Policy Review, May 2009.

enhance national and homeland security. The Cyber Security and Information Assurance (CSIA) program area focuses on R&D to prevent, resist, detect, respond to, and/or recover from actions that compromise or threaten to compromise the availability, integrity, or confidentiality of network-based systems.

NSF and DARPA have been two other leading sources of Federal telecommunications R&D support. NSF, a long-time supporter of telecommunications R&D that spans a range of topics, is currently emphasizing new approaches through such efforts as the Networking Technology and Systems (NeTS) program and the Global Environment for Network Innovations (GENI) experimental facility being planned by NSF in collaboration with the research community. DARPA has funded a number of important telecommunications advances in the past, including elements of the Internet itself.

The DHS S&T Directorate provides resources to improve homeland security by providing technology that helps the operating components of State, local, tribal, and territorial emergency responders. For example, The S&T Directorate's Command, Control, and Interoperability Division develops interoperable communications standards and protocols for emergency responders, cybersecurity tools for protecting the integrity of the Internet, and automated capabilities to recognize and analyze potential threats. Also, the Infrastructure and Geophysical Division focuses on identifying and mitigating the vulnerabilities of the 18 CIKR sectors.

NCS is working toward the goal of providing national security and emergency users with access to the converged information services of next-generation networks in a manner that provides a high likelihood of service success during disasters and other events that cause public users to experience severe degradation or loss of communications services. NCSD—working with research organizations, critical infrastructure operators, and infrastructure developers—plans, coordinates, manages, and conducts activities to secure cyberspace. These activities include roadmap development, research program management, test beds, and experimentation and exercise development. NCSD has identified two overarching objectives: (1) build and maintain an effective national cyberspace response system, and (2) implement a cyber risk management program for the protection of critical infrastructure. NCS and NCSD participate in the NITRD program. NCS also works closely with NCSD to coordinate communications and cyber R&D requirements for submission to the DHS S&T Directorate, the primary R&D arm of DHS.

As in other science, technology, and engineering fields of critical importance to the Nation, Federal leadership should energize a broad collaboration with private sector partners and stakeholders in academia and in national and industry laboratories. The Federal Government should provide a framework for R&D strategies that focus on game-changing technologies that will help meet infrastructure objectives, building on the existing NITRD strategies and other R&D-related work. The Federal Government should greatly expand coordination of these strategies with industry and academic research efforts to avoid duplication, leverage and synchronize complementary capabilities and agendas, and ensure that technology transitions and enters into the marketplace.

7.2 Sector R&D Requirements

Infrastructure must be resilient against physical damage, unauthorized manipulation, and electronic assault. In addition to protection of the information itself, a risk mitigation strategy for cyberspace must focus on the devices used to access the infrastructure; the services provided by the infrastructure; supporting elements of the networks; and all means of moving, storing, and processing information. In this environment of heightened risk, the Federal Government has a role to play in R&D coordination and in setting requirements. The communications system itself might bear the brunt of events and must have resilience or the capability to recover in order to manage a response and preserve governmental functions.

DHS is working toward the goal of providing NS/EP users with access to the converged information services of NGNs. The R&D requirements include:

- Develop a coordinated plan for national security and emergency preparedness communications capabilities over next-generation networks, including milestones and funding requirements;

- Develop options for additional services that the Federal Government could acquire, or direct investments that the government could make in the information and communications infrastructure to enhance the survivability of communications during a time of natural disaster, crisis, or conflict;

- Develop technologies to facilitate alert and warning messages to the public; and

- Coordinate with international partners and standards bodies to support next-generation NS/EP communications capabilities in a globally distributed next-generation environment.

The CSIA R&D Plan responded to recent calls for improved Federal CSIA R&D.[14] Developed by the CSIA Interagency Working Group (IWG), an organization under the National Science and Technology Council (NSTC), the plan provides baseline information and a technical framework for coordinated multiagency R&D in CSIA. The following strategic Federal objectives for CSIA R&D are derived from a review of current legislative and regulatory policy requirements, analyses of cybersecurity threats and infrastructure vulnerabilities, and agency mission requirements:

- Support RDT&E of CSIA technologies aimed at preventing, protecting against, detecting, responding to, and recovering from cyber attacks that may have large-scale consequences;

- Address CSIA R&D needs that are unique to critical infrastructure;

- Develop and accelerate the deployment of new communications protocols that better ensure the security of information transmitted over networks;

- Support the establishment of experimental environments such as test beds that allow government, academic, and industry researchers to conduct a broad range of CSIA development and assessment activities;

- Provide a foundation for the long-term goal of economically informed, risk-based CSIA decisionmaking; and

- Provide novel and next-generation secure concepts and architectures through long-term research.

The identification of requirements calls for a comprehensive assessment of the progress and impact of current initiatives and a forward-thinking perspective on future needs. To enhance U.S. competitiveness, the Federal Government should work with industry to develop migration paths and incentives for the rapid adoption of research and technology development, including encouragement of collaboration between academic and industrial laboratories.

IPAWS will participate in and take advantage of the sector's R&D efforts to provide reliable and secure communications technologies to ensure its mission of providing alert and warning messages to the American public.

In addition to R&D requirements that support secure communications pathways, IPAWS has the following R&D requirements:

- Provide audio and visual formats for alert and warning message dissemination to accommodate persons with auditory and visual disabilities;

- Provide audio and visual formats for alert and warning message dissemination to those for whom English is not their primary language; and

- Provide for the survivability of the alert and warning dissemination system.

---

[14] Outlined in the following documents: (1) the OSTP/OMB Memorandum on Administration FY 2007 R&D Budget Priorities, (2) Cyber Security: A Crisis of Prioritization, the 2005 report of the President's Information Technology Advisory Committee (PITAC), (3) the 2003 National Strategy to Secure Cyberspace, and (4) the 2002 Cyber Security Research and Development Act (Public Law (P.L.) 107-305).

7.3 Sector R&D Plan

To provide a starting point and framework for a coordinated interagency R&D plan to improve the stability and security of the communications infrastructure, the following baseline information reflects the criteria used to select new and existing R&D initiatives. The plan must identify technical priorities in which there may be investment opportunities for the sector. Together, the technical and funding priorities set the stage for the development of a sector R&D roadmap. Planning and conducting Communications Sector R&D will require concerted Federal activities on several fronts, as well as collaboration with the private sector. The specifics of the strategy proposed in the sector R&D plan are described in the following recommendations:

- Target R&D investments toward strategic needs that address and complement areas in which the private sector is productively engaged;

- Focus on threats with the greatest potential impact, as well as investigation of innovative approaches toward increasing the overall security and dependability of communications systems;

- Require sustained coordination and collaboration among agencies;

- Promote agency participation in interagency and cross-sector R&D coordination and collaboration on an ongoing basis;

- Build in security from the beginning;

- Support fundamental R&D that explores inherently more secure next-generation technologies; and

- Assess the security implications of emerging technologies and the potential impact of R&D results on new technologies as they emerge, such as cloud computing.

7.4 R&D Management Processes

The R&D management process requires a structured approach that involves identifying and translating needs into measurable and relevant requirements and implementing a quality assurance framework that will guarantee that these requirements are consistently met. The R&D management processes are analyzed, refined, and redesigned to ensure fulfillment of those requirements. The management process utilizes quantitative methods to ensure that design and service specifications, standard operating procedures (SOPs), and other requirements are traceable back to the R&D requirements and plan. When properly implemented, the management process becomes a major driver of the quality assurance and engineering activities within the R&D plan. This is important because requirements should directly drive core processes within CIKR protection R&D. More importantly:

- Agencies should use the R&D plan's technical priorities to work with the private sector to develop a roadmap of sector R&D priorities; this effort should emphasize coordinated agency activities that address gaps and should accelerate the development of strategic capabilities.

- Federal agencies should develop and implement a multiagency plan to support R&D for a new generation of methods and technologies for cost-effectively measuring component, network, and system security.

- The Federal Government should institute more effective coordination by engaging the private sector in efforts to better understand each other's views of Communications Sector cybersecurity and R&D needs, priorities, and investments.

- Federal agencies should improve communication and coordination with operators of both Federal and private sector critical infrastructure who have shared interests. Information exchange and outreach activities that accelerate technology transition should be integral parts of Federal R&D activities.

- The Federal Government should foster a broad partnership of government, industry, research, and private sector users to develop, test, and deploy more secure next-generation networks.

8. Manage and Coordinate SSA Responsibilities

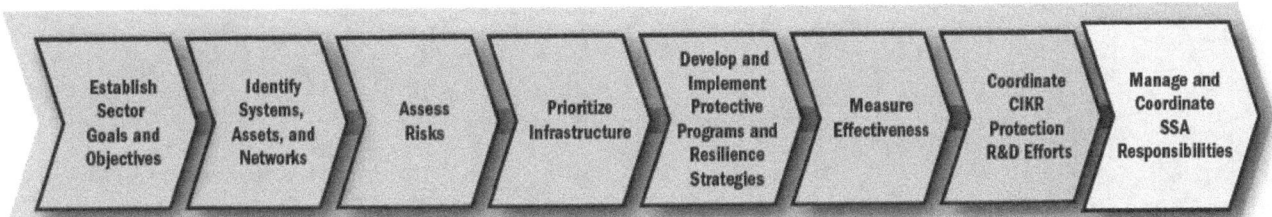

As the SSA for the Communications Sector, NCS manages the industry-government relationship to reduce risk to the Communications Sector. NCS does this by coordinating mitigation activities with Communications Sector partners. This chapter presents an overview of the NCS program management approach. Specifically, this section further discusses implementation of the partnership model and information sharing mechanisms. NCS manages and coordinates the processes of the SSP, which include SSP maintenance, updates, and training and education. While all SSA responsibilities are managed through NCS, most activities will involve extensive industry, government, and sector partner collaboration.

8.1 The Program Management Approach

The Communications Sector approach to managing risk and associated CIKR protection efforts within the sector requires NCS to support and strengthen industry and government partnerships continually and to ensure that these entities build resilience and redundancy into the Nation's communications infrastructure. The existing structure of NCS supports its current mission under E.O. 12472 to "Assist the President, the National Security Council, the Director of the Office of Science and Technology Policy, and the Director of the Office of Management and Budget in (1) the exercise of the communications functions and responsibilities, and (2) the coordination of the planning for and provision of [NS/EP] communications for the Federal Government under all circumstances, including crisis or emergency, attack, and recovery and reconstitution." This mission continues to be met by establishing and maintaining robust industry partnerships and programs and new partnerships with Federal, State, local, tribal, and international entities. Two successful collaborative partnerships, the NCC and NSIEs, have proven how effectively industry and government can work together to reduce the risk to the Communications Sector. Because the NCS mission already is aligned with its infrastructure protection and NS/EP communications responsibilities and its preferred approach for executing those responsibilities, it is most appropriate for NCS to assimilate its NIPP-related responsibilities into its existing structure.

NCS will manage its responsibilities as the Communications SSA primarily through the NCS GIP&M Branch, although specific responsibilities may be allocated to other offices within NCS as appropriate. The NCS GIP&M Branch will manage most of the key processes and partnerships associated with the implementation of the NIPP risk management framework. This effort will allow NCS to ensure that the NIPP-related responsibilities always are conducted by the most appropriate entity and will create a centralized point of distribution for work with other Federal, State, local, tribal, international, and private sector partners. In addition, NCS will maintain an active dialogue with the CGCC and the CSCC to monitor the execution of these responsibilities. Table 8-1 identifies primary task responsibilities for specific divisions of NCS.

Table 8-1: Program Management Responsibilities

Task	Responsible NCS Branch
Priority Services Technology Assessment	NCS Technology and Programs
Planning for and Coordinating Response and Reconstitution Training and Education Risk Assessment	NCS Critical Infrastructure Protection
Communications Sector Management Partnerships and Outreach CSSP Maintenance and Sector Reporting	NCS Government-Industry Planning & Management
Resources and Budget	NCS Plans and Resources

8.2 Processes and Responsibilities

CSSP Maintenance and Update

The NCS GIP&M Branch, in its role as the overall manager of NCS SSA-related responsibilities, is responsible for maintaining the CSSP. The CSSP is reviewed annually to ensure that it reflects current sector processes, as well as the continuously evolving nature of the risk environment. This annual review will occur as part of the sector's annual reporting process. As NCS works with its sector partners to produce this annual report, it will also work with them to identify any changes in process or sector characteristics that may have occurred over the preceding year. During this annual review, the CSSP is updated as appropriate. On a triennial basis, a complete review of the CSSP is conducted following the update of the NIPP. The CSSP builds on risk management initiatives and activities on which the sector has embarked during the past three years. The plan also will be reviewed after any incident or exercise event that has a major impact on the sector. In addition, the Communications Sector will coordinate closely with the IT Sector to develop the next version of the CSSP.

In addition to conducting these periodic reviews, the NCS GIP&M Branch will be responsible for identifying any changes in processes associated with the NIPP risk management framework or in the characteristics of the sector. In the case of a major change to an element of the CSSP, a decision will be made to update the CSSP outside the normal annual review cycle. In all cases, revisions to the CSSP will be coordinated with sector partners and will be reviewed by the CGCC and the CSCC.

CSSP Implementation Milestones

As directed in HSPD-7 and further described in the NIPP, Sector Annual Reports are produced by each sector annually to identify, prioritize, and coordinate CIKR protection progress and requirements in their respective sectors. This report, which is submitted to DHS, describes the sector's CIKR protection goals, priorities, programs progress, and related resource requirements. Sector RMAs are also detailed within this annual report to highlight and provide specific examples of how the sector continues to progress with respect to CIKR protection.

The production of the Communications Sector Annual Report is managed by NCS but involves input from all stakeholders within the Communications Sector. The process used to gather input from sector partners is the same that is used to produce the CSSP. When appropriate, the CGCC and the CSCC will meet to provide input to the annual report and to ensure that the report's data accurately reflects an evolving CIKR risk management effort with an emphasis on all hazards, protection, resilience, and risk mitigation of CIKR protection activities sector-wide. In addition, CGCC and CSCC members review the annual report before it is submitted to DHS to ensure that all relevant data are included. Other sector partners also contribute to the production of the annual report, including State and local entities.

The Communications Sector has made significant progress in completing specific actions and milestones in pursuit of closing capability gaps. The Communications Sector accomplished this by aligning existing CIKR protective programs and risk management decisions with seven goals, as outlined within the 2007 CSSP, in addition to enhancing the foundation for protective programs through collaboration with sector partners.

Training and Education

NCS recognizes the need for training and education in all areas of the NIPP risk management framework. A large portion of this training is targeted toward NCS staff members who are responsible for implementing the processes outlined in the CSSP. This includes specialized training on risk management methodologies related to physical and cybersecurity risk assessments for those who are responsible for ensuring that limited resources are effectively applied. GIP&M staff members are required to complete mandatory training in critical infrastructure protection and programs. Often, training is available through traditional employee training, although as the CSSP is implemented, there will be a need for expertise in areas where existing training avenues do not suffice. As this need arises, NCS will seek appropriate sources for this training to ensure that all necessary capabilities are adequately developed.

In addition to individual employee training and education, education for providers and users of NS/EP communications is a critical factor in the success of the implementation of this CSSP. As such, NCS facilitates and participates in various programs that are aimed at building awareness or educating a larger community about the problem of ensuring the functioning of critical infrastructure and the availability of NCS programs and activities such as the NS/EP Priority Telecommunications Service (PTS) program. NS/EP PTS enhances the ability of NS/EP users to complete calls through a degraded PSTN using WPS during a crisis or emergency situation. The Route Diversity Forum periodically helps educate NCS member departments and agencies about improving communications resilience. NCS will build on this effort or initiate new ones to ensure proper scope and reach. Overall, a key first step in implementing a successful protection strategy is elevating national awareness. Toward that end, NCS will intensify its efforts to conduct outreach and develop industry and government partnerships, which have proven to be vital for protecting communications infrastructure. NCS will continue to develop a strategic program for marketing NCS and its products and services to its Federal customers; the broader NS/EP community at the State, local, tribal, and territorial levels; and the private sector.

NCS also will work with other sectors to improve their communications resilience. To reach out to the broadcast industry, NCS will work through the FCC, trade associations, and the FCC Media Security and Reliability Council (MSRC), which is developing best practices to ensure the optimal reliability, robustness, and security of broadcast facilities. NCS also is reaching out to other sectors with which it shares interdependencies and is assisting them in reviewing how their plans address communications interdependencies.

8.3 Implementing the Partnership Model

Coordinating Structures

NCS, as the SSA for the Communications Sector, is responsible for coordinating the development and implementation of the sector's GCC and for coordinating and collaborating with the SCC. This subsection describes the CIKR protection-related coordinating structures and mechanisms used within the Communications Sector. It also highlights the role of State and local entities in sector operations and the potential interconnectedness of U.S. CIKR with foreign countries.

NIPP Coordination Councils

Communications Government Coordinating Council. The CGCC helps coordinate the implementation of the NIPP and the corresponding CSSP across government and between government and the Communications Sector. Membership in the CGCC includes DHS (NCS, OEC, and NCSD), DOC, DoD (the Office of the Secretary of Defense/Networks and Information Integration), the FCC, the General Services Administration, NTIA, DOJ, and NARUC. NCS is the chair of the CGCC.

Communications Sector Coordinating Council. The CSCC, an industry-only body with more than 25 communications companies and trade associations, assists in implementing the CSSP and provides input on critical infrastructure protection and sector-related policies and programs. The CSCC is not operational, but focuses on input to critical infrastructure protection policies and plans. As such, it will not take on all of the responsibilities that NIPP designates to SCCs. The NCC will continue to coordinate operational issues.

State, Local, Tribal, and Territorial Government Entities. NCS can facilitate improved coordination among State, local, tribal, and territorial authorities and the communications industry on CIKR protection initiatives through the SLTTGCC within the CIPAC framework. NCS will develop a process to facilitate coordination among State and local authorities and the communications industry on CIKR protection initiatives, including collecting critical sector asset listings and vulnerability or impact assessments. Through NARUC, NCS will work to build on outreach to States on key issues (e.g., pandemic preparedness, access, and credentialing) and provide POCs to the NARUC/FCC communications assurance emergency POC network.

Continuity Communications Managers Group (CCMG). This is an NCS-sponsored quarterly Federal interagency communications conference for the contingency communications community. It is a forum for interagency exchange of issues, ideas, and problems. CCMG serves as a body to facilitate the compliance with NCS Directive 3-10.

Regional Communications Coordinators (RCCs). RCCs are NCS staff designated to support geographic regions of the country in order to promote priority services communications programs to emergency response organizations and State and local leaders, and to coordinate with State and local government officials on emergency communications policy, training, and operations. In 2010 the RCCs are being replaced with Communications Liaisons, who will have similar responsibilities.

International

NCS participates in international organizations and bilateral discussions with other countries regarding the NCS model for Communications Sector coordination and infrastructure protection. These partnerships are described below.

U.S./Canada Civil Emergency Planning Telecommunications Advisory Group (CEPTAG). CEPTAG was established in 1988 to provide a forum for addressing concerns and enabling cross-border cooperation and mutual assistance during an emergency. NCS, OEC, and their industry partners are actively involved in interdependency issues through CEPTAG to address communications concerns that are common to each nation. CEPTAG is a permanent U.S.-Canadian government exchange that provides awareness, advice, and assistance to other specialized U.S.-Canadian Emergency Planning Committees and Working Groups on cross-border telecommunications requirements for emergency response.

Security and Prosperity Partnership (SPP). SPP, launched in June 2005, builds on existing relationships among the United States, Canada, and Mexico by providing a framework to advance collaboration. SPP created architecture to enhance further the security of North America while simultaneously promoting its citizens' economic well-being.

The three governments have established numerous goals and initiatives, with corresponding deadlines, as well as various working groups to address cross-border issues.

The NATO Civil Communications Planning Committee (CCPC). The NATO CCPC is responsible for ensuring the continued availability of civil communications during crises and war for civil and military purposes. CCPC provides for the maintenance of communication services for political, economic, and military purposes, including communications and postal facilities/services. CCPC creates work programs based on comprehensive political and ministerial guidance and works to advance the civil emergency planning and response capabilities of the alliance.

U.S./United Kingdom (U.K.) Joint Contact Group (JCG). The initiatives of the U.S./U.K. NS/EP communications relationship are pursued primarily through the JCG. NCS leads the Communications Sector work, and its primary partner is the U.K.'s Central Sponsor for Information Assurance. The principal task being conducted under the auspices of the JCG is the development of government-to-government priority routing capabilities for emergency communications.

International Telecommunication Union (ITU). NCS represents U.S. Government interests at the ITU. The ITU, under the auspices of the UN, has 189 member states and more than 650 industry sector members. The ITU serves as the world's principal communications standards organization and explores topics such as NGNs and international emergency preference schemes.

Critical Foreign Dependencies Initiative. The Critical Foreign Dependencies Initiative is designed to identify assets and systems that are critical to the Nation's public health, economy, or homeland/national security, but are located outside of the United States. The initiative focuses on identifying critical foreign dependencies for both protection and incident response purposes within three categories: (1) direct physical dependencies, (2) sole or predominantly foreign-sourced goods, and (3) critical supply chain nodes.

8.4 Information Sharing and Protection

Information-Sharing Mechanisms

The effective implementation of the NIPP is predicated on active participation by industry and government partners in robust multidirectional information sharing. When owners and operators are provided with a comprehensive picture of threats or hazards to CIKR and participate in ongoing multidirectional information flow, their ability to assess risks, make prudent security investments, and develop appropriate resilience strategies is substantially enhanced. Similarly, when the government is equipped with infrastructure information from industry, it can better analyze, synthesize, and disseminate threat information accordingly.

The NIPP information-sharing network approach constitutes a shift from a strictly hierarchical model to a networked model, allowing distribution and access to information both vertically and horizontally, as well as the ability to enable decentralized decisionmaking and actions. The objectives of the network approach are as follows:

• Enable secure multidirectional information sharing between and across industry and government that focuses, streamlines, and reduces redundant reporting to the greatest extent possible;

• Implement a common set of all-hazards communications, coordination, and information-sharing capabilities for all industry and government partners;

• Protect the integrity and confidentiality of sensitive information;

- Enable the multidirectional flow of information that is required by sector partners to assess risks, conduct risk management activities, invest in security measures, and allocate resources;

- Set a path for State, local, tribal, territorial, and private sector partners to be integrated, as appropriate, into the intelligence cycle, including the provision of input to the development of collection requirements; and

- Provide sector partners with a comprehensive common operating picture that includes timely and accurate information about natural hazards, general and specific terrorist threats, incidents and events, impact assessments, and best practices.

One of the primary goals of information sharing within the Communications Sector is to communicate both actionable information on threats and incidents and information pertaining to overall CIKR status (e.g., plausible threats, cyber threats, vulnerabilities, potential consequences, incident situations, and recovery progress) so that owners and operators, States, localities, tribal governments, and other sector partners can assess risks, make appropriate security investments, and take effective and efficient protective actions. The end result of an effective environment for information sharing is to provide timely and relevant information that partners can use to make decisions and take the necessary actions to manage CIKR risk.

Information sharing in the Communications Sector occurs largely through established channels among NCS, including HITRAC, C-ISAC, the National Infrastructure Coordinating Center (NICC), the NOC, NSIEs, and the Partnership and Outreach Division (POD).

- **The Homeland Infrastructure Threat Risk Analysis Center (HITRAC):** HITRAC integrates the infrastructure analysis capabilities of the Office of Intelligence and Analysis and the DHS Office of Infrastructure Protection, providing actionable all hazards, risk informed analysis and strategies for Federal, State, local, tribal, territorial, private sector, and international partners. HITRAC manages NISAC to ensure the development of a comprehensive infrastructure analysis program for DHS and the Nation, and coordinates decision support during incidents and periods of heightened alert. Congress mandates that NISAC serve as a source of national expertise to address critical infrastructure protection research and analysis. NISAC combines the infrastructure analysis capabilities of Los Alamos and Sandia National Laboratories. These two centers form the backbone of the Department's infrastructure-related analysis, providing a comprehensive suite of analytical capabilities and developmental activities.

- **NCS/NCC Communications Information Sharing and Analysis Center (C-ISAC):** The NCC assists NCS in the initiation, coordination, restoration, and reconstitution of NS/EP communications services or facilities under all conditions of crisis or emergency. The NCC regularly monitors the status of communications systems. It collects situational and operational information on a regular basis, as well as during a crisis, and provides information to NCS. NCS, in turn, shares information with the White House and other DHS components. NCC Watch is a 24/7, 365 days per year service that is collocated with US-CERT in the NCCIC. Both entities work closely together to share situational and operational information on a regular basis. This information exchange is a vital component for ensuring the protective posture of both the Communications and IT Sectors. ISACs provide an example of an effective private sector information-sharing and analysis mechanism. ISACs are sector-specific entities that advance physical and cyber CIKR protection efforts by establishing and maintaining frameworks for operational interaction between and among members and external sector partners.

- **National Infrastructure Coordinating Center (NICC):** The NICC is a 24/7 watch/operations center that maintains ongoing operational and situational awareness of the Nation's CIKR sectors. As a CIKR-focused element of the NOC, the NICC provides a centralized mechanism and process for information sharing and coordination among the Government, SCCs, GCCs, and other industry partners. The NICC receives situational, operational, and incident information from the CIKR sectors in accordance with the information-sharing protocols established in the NRF. The Homeland Security Information Network (HSIN) is the NICC's primary system for disseminating information to the CIKR sectors. The NICC also disseminates products originated by HITRAC that contain all-hazards warning, threat, and CIKR protection information.

- **National Operations Center (NOC):** The NOC, formerly known as the Homeland Security Operations Center, serves as the Nation's hub for domestic incident management operational coordination and situational awareness. The NOC facilitates homeland security information sharing and operational coordination among Federal, State, local, tribal, and private sector partners, as well as select members of the international community. As such, it is at the center of the NIPP information-sharing network.

- **Network Security Information Exchanges (NSIEs):** Since 1991, the NSTAC NSIE and the Federal Government NSIE have worked together to share information that addresses network security concerns. NSIEs meet jointly every two months. Together, NSIEs provide a working forum for identifying issues that involve unauthorized penetration or manipulation of PN software and databases that affect national security and NS/EP communications. NSIEs periodically conduct risk assessments of the PN.

- **Partnership and Outreach Division (POD):** POD's mission is to develop and sustain public-private partnerships, sector expertise, and information-sharing tools and processes to facilitate coordination within and across CIKR sectors, and to promote operational, situational, and strategic cross-sector operational and risk awareness. Additionally, POD is charged with oversight of the NIPP and its management and implementation processes. POD fulfills its mission by managing and supporting the CIKR partnership framework; facilitating and supporting private sector and government operational information-sharing and activities coordination; providing interface and liaison assistance with Federal, State, and local government and private sector CIKR partners; and providing CIKR education, training, and outreach support.

The NIPP supports the broad concept of a multidirectional networked information-sharing approach. DHS has designated HSIN-Critical Sectors (HSIN-CS) to be its primary information-sharing platform between the critical infrastructure key resource sectors. HSIN-CS enables DHS and critical sector stakeholders to communicate, coordinate, and share information in support of the sector partnership model. Through HSIN-CS, users are able to:

- Receive, submit, and discuss timely, actionable, and accurate information;

- Communicate information pertaining to threats, vulnerabilities, security, response, and recovery activities that affect sector and cross-sector operations; and

- Maintain a direct, trusted channel with DHS and other vetted sector stakeholders.

A major objective of HSIN-CS is to share information to generate effective risk management decisions and to encourage collaboration and coordination on plans, strategies, protective measures, resilience, and response/recovery.

In addition to sharing information through already established channels, Communications Sector industry and government partners regularly work together on ad hoc projects and protective programs, which offer additional opportunities for successful information sharing. Specific programs in place that address Internet security and communications and IT cross-sector issues are US-CERT, CSCSWG, the National Cyber Response Coordination Group (NCRCG), and NET Guard. These information-sharing mechanisms are described in chapter 5.

Data Protection Mechanisms

Wherever possible, information shared among any entities will be protected through the appropriate mechanisms. In cases where information is shared among government entities, data will carry the appropriate classification markings and will be handled accordingly. In cases where data are exchanged between industry and government, it will receive similar protections where possible (e.g., "commercial proprietary" markings or contractor nondisclosure agreements).

Appendix A: List of Acronyms and Abbreviations

APEC	Asia-Pacific Economic Cooperation
ATM	Asynchronous Transfer Mode
BCP	Business Continuity Planning
BSC	Base Station Controller
BSS	Broadcast Satellite Service
CATV	Cable Television
CCMG	Continuity Communications Managers Group
CCPC	Civil Communications Planning Committee
CDEP Report	Communications Dependency on Electric Power Report
CDEPWG	Communications Dependency on Electric Power Working Group
CEPTAG	Civil Emergency Planning Telecommunications Advisory Group
CERT	Computer Emergency Readiness Team
CGCC	Communications Government Coordinating Council
CII	Critical Infrastructure Information
CIPAC	Critical Infrastructure Partnership Advisory Council
C-ISAC	Communications Information Sharing and Analysis Center
CIKR	Critical Infrastructure and Key Resources
CLEC	Competitive Local Exchange Carrier
CMRS	Commercial Mobile Radio Services
COG	Continuity of Government
CONUS	Continental United States
COOP	Continuity of Operations
COP	Committee of Principals
COR	Council of Representatives
CSCC	Communications Sector Coordinating Council

CSCSWG	Cross-Sector Cyber Security Working Group
CSIA	Cyber Security and Information Assurance
CSIA IWG	Cyber Security and Information Assurance Interagency Working Group
CSRIC	Communications Security, Reliability, and Interoperability Council
CSSP	Communications Sector-Specific Plan
DARPA	Defense Advanced Research Projects Agency
DEC	Disaster Emergency Communications
DHS	U.S. Department of Homeland Security
DIRS	Disaster Information Reporting System
DOC	U.S. Department of Commerce
DoD	U.S. Department of Defense
DOJ	U.S. Department of Justice
DOS	U.S. Department of State
DPAS	Defense Priorities and Allocations System
DSL	Digital Subscriber Line
DTV	Digital Television
E-911	Enhanced 911
EAS	Emergency Alert System
EC	Executive Committee
ECG	Enduring Constitutional Government
ECPC	Emergency Communications Preparedness Center
E.O.	Executive Order
EOP	Executive Office of the President
EOT	Emergency Operations Team
ERC	Emergency Response Council
ERT	Emergency Response Training
ESF-2	Emergency Support Function 2
FCC	Federal Communications Commission
FEMA	Federal Emergency Management Agency
FPIC	Federal Partnership for Interoperable Communications
FY	Fiscal Year
GCC	Government Coordinating Council
GEO	Geostationary Earth Orbiter
GETS	Government Emergency Telecommunications Service
GIP&M	Government-Industry Planning and Management

GPS	Global Positioning System
HF	High Frequency
HFC	Hybrid Fiber Coaxial
HITRAC	Homeland Infrastructure Threat and Risk Analysis Center
HSA	Homeland Security Advisor
HSIN	Homeland Security Information Network
HSIN-CS	Homeland Security Information Network–Critical Sectors
HSPD	Homeland Security Presidential Directive
IAC	Internet Analysis Capability
ICTAP	Interoperable Communications Technical Assistance Program
IMA	Individual Mobilization Augmentee
IMS	Internet-protocol Multimedia Subsystem
IP	Internet Protocol
IPAWS	Integrated Public Alert and Warning System
IR	Industry Requirements
IRI	Industrial Research Institute
ISAC	Information Sharing and Analysis Center
ISDN	Integrated Services Digital Network
ISP	Internet Service Provider
IT	Information Technology
IT-ISAC	Information Technology Information Sharing and Analysis Center
ITU	International Telecommunication Union
IXC	Interexchange Carrier
JCG	Joint Contact Group
JFO	Joint Field Office
LATA	Local Access and Transport Areas
LEC	Local Exchange Carrier
LEO	Low Earth Orbit
LERG	Local Exchange Routing Guide
MEF	Mission Essential Function
MEO	Middle Earth Orbit
MG	Media Gateway
MGC	Media Gateway Controller
MSC	Mobile Switching Center
MS-ISAC	Multi-State Information Sharing and Analysis Center

MSO	Multiple-System Operators
MSRC	Media Security and Reliability Council
MSS	Mobile Satellite Service
MVPD	Multichannel Video Programming Distribution
NARUC	National Association of Regulatory Utility Commissioners
NATO	North Atlantic Treaty Organization
NCC	National Coordinating Center
NCCIC	National Cybersecurity and Communications Integration Center
NCIPP	National Critical Infrastructure Prioritization Program
NCIRP	National Cyber Incident Response Plan
NCRCG	National Cyber Response Coordination Group
NCS	National Communications System
NCS COP	National Communications System Committee of Principals
NCSD	National Cyber Security Division
NDAC	Network Design and Analysis Capability
NECP	National Emergency Communications Plan
NEF	National Essential Function
NENA	National Emergency Number Association
NGN	Next-Generation Network
NGPS	Next-Generation Priority Service
NICC	National Infrastructure Coordinating Center
NIPP	National Infrastructure Protection Plan
NISAC	National Infrastructure Simulation and Analysis Center
NIST	National Institute of Standards and Technology
NITRD	Networking and Information Technology Research and Development
NLE	National Level Exercise
NOC	National Operations Center
NPTS	National Plan for Telecommunications Support in Non-Wartime Emergencies
NRF	National Response Framework
NRSC	Network Reliability Steering Committee
NS/EP	National Security and Emergency Preparedness
NSF	National Science Foundation
NSIE	Network Security Information Exchange
NSRA	National Sector Risk Assessment
NSSE	National Special Security Event

NSTAC	National Security Telecommunications Advisory Committee
NSTC	National Science and Technology Council
NTIA	National Telecommunications and Information Administration
OAS	Organization of American States
OEC	Office of Emergency Communications
OIC	Office for Interoperability and Compatibility
OMB	Office of Management and Budget
OSTP	Office of Science and Technology Policy
PBX	Private Branch Exchange
PCII	Protected Critical Infrastructure Information
PCIS	Partnership for Critical Infrastructure Security
PDD	Presidential Decision Directive
PMEF	Primary Mission Essential Function
PITAC	President's Information Technology Advisory Committee
P.L.	Public Law
PN	Public Network
POC	Point of Contact
POD	Partnership and Outreach Division
POP	Point of Presence
PSA	Protective Security Advisor
PSAP	Public Safety Answering Point
PSTN	Public Switched Telephone Network
PTS	Priority Telecommunications Service
PUC	Public Utility Commission
R&D	Research and Development
RCC	Regional Communication Coordinator
RDM	Route Diversity Methodology
RDT&E	Research, Development, Testing, and Evaluation
RDTF	Research and Development Task Force
RDX	R&D Exchange
RMA	Risk Mitigation Activity
RRAP	Regional Resilience Assessment Program
SCC	Sector Coordinating Council
SCIP	Statewide Communication Interoperability Plan
SG	Signaling Gateway

SHARES	Shared Resources
SHIRA	Strategic Homeland Infrastructure Risk Assessment
SME	Subject Matter Expert
SONET	Synchronous Optical Network
SOP	Standard Operating Procedure
SPP	Security and Prosperity Partnership of North America
SRAS	Special Routing Arrangement Service
SS7	Signaling System 7
SSA	Sector-Specific Agency
SSP	Sector-Specific Plan
S&T	Science and Technology Directorate
STL	Studio-to-Transmitter Link
SWIC	Statewide Interoperability Coordinator
TEPI Report	Report to the President on Telecommunications and Electric Power Interdependencies: The Implications of Long-Term Outages
TSP	Telecommunications Service Priority
TT&C	Telemetry, Tracking, and Command
TTX	Tabletop Exercise
U.K.	United Kingdom
UN	United Nations
U.S.	United States
U.S.C.	United States Code
US-CERT	United States Computer Emergency Readiness Team
USDA	U.S. Department of Agriculture
VoIP	Voice Over Internet Protocol
VSAT	Very Small Aperture Terminal
WPS	Wireless Priority Service

Appendix B: Glossary of Key Terms

Asset. Person, structure, facility, information, material, or process that has value. This includes contracts, facilities, property, records, unobligated or unexpended balances of appropriations, and other funds or resources, personnel, intelligence, technology, or physical infrastructure, or anything useful that contributes to the success of something, such as an organizational mission. Assets are items of value or properties to which value can be assigned. From an intelligence standpoint, assets include any resource—person, group, relationship, instrument, installation, or supply—at the disposal of an intelligence organization for use in an operational or support role.

Communications Architecture Elements. Assets, systems, and networks that make up the communications architecture. The following are sample categories of architecture elements:

Core Network/Internet Backbone. The portion of the communications network that consists of high-capacity network elements servicing nationwide, regional, and international connectivity.

Signaling and Control Systems. Systems that exchange information regarding the establishment of a connection and control the management of the network.

Shared Assets and Systems. Assets and systems owned and operated by multiple companies, including facilities where equipment is collocated and systems are shared by network operators.

Access. Primarily the local portion of the network connecting end users to the backbone that enables users to send or receive communications. Access includes equipment and systems such as Public Switched Telephone Network (PSTN) switches, asynchronous transfer mode (ATM) switches, video servers for video on demand, and Internet Protocol (IP) routers for Internet Service Providers (ISPs).

Customer Equipment. Equipment owned and operated by the end user or located at the end user's facility. Customers include individuals, organizations, businesses, and government.

Communications Sector. Public and private sector entities that have equities in the provisioning, use, protection, or regulation of communications networks and services. The Communications Sector is made up of five industry sectors:

Wireline. Consists primarily of the PSTN, but also includes enterprise networks. The PSTN is a domestic communications network accessed by telephones, key telephone systems, private branch exchange (PBX) trunks, and data arrangements. Despite the industry's transition to packet-based networks, the traditional PSTN remains the backbone of the communications infrastructure. Includes landline telephone, the Internet, and submarine cable infrastructure.

Wireless. Refers to telecommunication in which electromagnetic waves (rather than some form of wire) carry the signal over part of or the entire communication path. Consists of cellular phone, paging, personal communication services, high-frequency radio, unlicensed wireless, and other commercial and private radio services.

Satellite. This is a space vehicle launched into orbit to relay audio, data, or video signals as part of a telecommunications network. Signals are transmitted to the satellite from earth station antennas, amplified, and sent back to earth for reception by other earth station antennas. Satellites are capable of linking two points, one point with many others, or multiple locations with other multiple locations. Uses a combination of terrestrial and space components to deliver various communications, Internet data, and video services.

Cable. This wireline network offers television, Internet, and voice services that interconnect with the PSTN through end offices. Primary cable television (CATV) network components include headends and fiber optic and/or HFC. Because the CATV network was designed primarily for downstream transmission of television signals, most of the existing network is being refitted to support two-way data transmissions.

Broadcasting. Broadcasting systems consist of free, over-the-air radio and television stations that offer analog and digital audio and video programming services and data services. Broadcasting has been the principal means of providing emergency alerting services to the public for six decades. Broadcasting systems operate in three frequency bands: medium frequency (MF (AM radio)), very high frequency (VHF (FM radio and television)), and ultra-high frequency (UHF (television)). The recent transition to digital television (DTV) and ongoing transition to digital radio provide broadcast stations with enhanced capabilities, including the ability to multicast multiple programs on a single channel.

Critical Infrastructure. As established in the National Infrastructure Protection Plan (NIPP), includes the following sectors: Agriculture and Food; Water; Dams; Healthcare and Public Health; Emergency Services; Government Facilities; Commercial Facilities; Defense Industrial Base; National Monuments and Icons; Information Technology; Communications; Energy; Nuclear Reactors, Materials, and Waste; Transportation Systems; Banking and Finance; Chemical; Critical Manufacturing; and Postal and Shipping.

Function. The service, process, capability, or operation performed by an asset, system, network, or organization.

Information Sharing. The exchange among entities or individuals of data, information, or knowledge stored within discrete information systems or created spontaneously using collaborative communication technologies.

Interdependency. Mutually reliant relationship between entities (objects, individuals, or groups). A relationship where the consequences of a positive or an adverse event affecting one will have cascading effects upon others.

Key Resources. Publicly or privately controlled asset necessary for the continuity of minimal government or economic operations or an asset that is of great historical significance to the Nation. An essential source of supply, support, information, or expertise; may be a physical asset (energy plant or other building), cyber in nature (World Wide Web/Internet), or human (intelligence) whose destruction would not necessarily endanger vital systems, but could create a local disaster or profoundly damage our Nation's morale or confidence.

Metrics. Quantifiable statements that support the performance measurement process by defining an element to be measured and indicating how that measurement will be taken. As used with regard to this document:

Descriptive Metrics. Used to understand sector resources and activities. They do not reflect CIKR protection performance.

Output (Process) Metrics. Measure whether specific activities were performed as planned, track the progression of a task, or report on the output of a process (e.g., inventorying assets). Process metrics show progress toward performing the activities necessary for achieving CIKR protection goals.

Outcome Metrics. Track progress toward a strategic goal by beneficial results instead of the level of activity, which indicates progress toward specific goals or objectives.

National Sector Risk Assessment. A process to collect and analyze consequences, vulnerabilities, and threats to the communications architecture to identify critical communications architectural elements at risk. The assessment is a collaborative effort with input from industry and government SMEs.

Nationally Critical Elements. Assets, systems, or networks that if destroyed, disrupted, or exploited would seriously threaten national security, result in catastrophic health effects or mass casualties, weaken the economy, or damage public morale and confidence.

Owners and Operators. Those entities responsible for day-to-day operations and investment in a particular asset, system, or network.

Prioritization. The process of using risk assessment results to identify where risk-reduction or mitigation efforts are most needed and subsequently determine which protective action should be instituted to realize the greatest effect.

Resilience. The ability to resist, absorb, and recover from or successfully adapt to adversity or a change in conditions. The communications infrastructure is, by design, resilient; however, other critical infrastructure sectors are responsible for achieving communications resilience by having an appropriate mix of diversity, redundancy, and recoverability based on a risk-based, cost-benefit assessment.

Diversity. Facilities should have diverse primary and backup communications capabilities that do not share common points of failure. Diversity solutions may include diverse data links (e.g., PSTN, satellite, and microwave), having local loops terminate at different central offices, obtaining services from different providers with certifiable diverse routes, or using alternative transport mechanisms (e.g., wireless, satellite).

*Redundancy.*Facilities should use multiple communications capabilities to sustain business operations and eliminate single points of failure that could disrupt primary services. Redundancy solutions include having multiple sites where a function is performed, multiple communications offices serving sites, and multiple routes between each site and the serving central offices.

Recoverability. Plans and processes should be in place to restore operations quickly if an interruption or failure occurs. Recoverability of network services could include network management controls, automatic service recovery technologies, and manual transfer to alternate facility routes.

Risk. The potential for an unwanted outcome resulting from an incident, event, or occurrence, as determined by its likelihood and the associated consequences. In the context of the NIPP, risk is the expected magnitude of loss as a result of a terrorist attack, natural disaster, or other incident, along with the likelihood of such an event occurring and causing that loss.

Threat. Natural or man-made occurrence, individual, entity, or action that has or indicates the potential to harm life, information, operations, the environment and/or property.

Vulnerability. Physical feature or operational attribute that renders an entity open to exploitation or susceptible to a given hazard.

Consequence. Effect of an event, incident, or occurrence.

Risk Assessment. Product or process which collects information and assigns values to risks for the purpose of informing priorities, developing or comparing courses of action, and informing decision making.

Risk Management Framework. As defined by the NIPP, the risk management framework is structured to promote continuous improvement to enhance CIKR protection by focusing activities on efforts to: set goals and objectives; identify assets, systems, and networks; assess risk based on consequences, vulnerabilities, and threats; establish priorities based on risk assessments and, increasingly, on return-on-investment for mitigating risk; implement protective programs and resiliency strategies; and measure effectiveness.

Value Proposition. A statement that outlines the national and homeland security interest in protecting the Nation's CIKR and articulates the benefits gained by all CIKR partners through the risk management framework and public-private partnership described in the NIPP.

Appendix C: Authorities

Key authorities for the Communications Sector address the availability, resilience, and security of the communications infrastructure and provide guidance on sector coordination and specific programs. This subsection gives brief summaries of the major authorities.

C.1 Broad Communications Infrastructure Protection Policies

- Homeland Security Presidential Directive 7 (HSPD-7) (December 2003): Assigns DHS lead responsibility for coordinating the protection of national critical infrastructure, including the Communications Sector. DHS has delegated to NCS the responsibility for coordinating protection of the Communications Sector.

- The Homeland Security Act of 2002 (November 2002): Under the act, DHS has issued an interim rule on Procedures for Handling Critical Infrastructure Information, which provides protection of such data that are voluntarily provided by the private sector.

- The National Strategy for the Physical Protection of Critical Infrastructure and Key Assets (July 2002): Directs DHS to work with the private sector to understand the risks associated with the physical vulnerabilities of CIKR, including the communications infrastructure.

- The National Strategy to Secure Cyberspace (July 2002): States that a top priority is to understand infrastructure interdependencies and improve the physical security of cyber systems and communications.

C.2 SSA Authorities

- E.O. 12472, Assignment of National Security and Emergency Preparedness Telecommunications Functions (April 3, 1984): Establishes NCS as the Federal interagency system for ensuring that the national telecommunications infrastructure is responsive to the NS/EP needs of the Federal Government, is capable of satisfying priority communications requirements, and is survivable under all circumstances. E.O. 12472 also establishes NCS as the focal point for joint industry-government NS/EP communications planning and directs the establishment of a national coordinating center.

- E.O. 12382, President's National Security Telecommunications Advisory Committee (September 13, 1982): Establishes NSTAC to provide top-level industry advice and expertise to the President on issues and problems related to implementing NS/EP communications policy.

- E.O. 12656, Assignment of Emergency Preparedness Responsibilities (November 18, 1988): Assigns Federal departments and agencies NS/EP responsibilities and directs them to develop plans and capabilities to ensure the continuity of essential operations.

- E.O. 13286, An Amendment of Executive Orders and Other Actions in Connection with the Transfer of Functions to the Secretary of Homeland Security (February 28, 2003): Amends several E.O.s, including E.O. 12472 and E.O. 12382, to account for the creation of DHS.

- National Security Decision Directive 97, National Security Telecommunications Policy (June 13, 1983): Outlines coordination between NCS, OSTP, and the Office of Management and Budget (OMB) to oversee the implementation of national security telecommunications policies. Also assigned specific responsibilities to the Manager of NCS, NSTAC, and other Federal departments and agencies.

- Presidential Decision Directive 67 (PDD-67), CLASSIFIED, (October 12, 1988): Relates to ECG, COOP planning, and COG operations. In addition, PDD-67 requires Federal agencies to develop COOP for essential operations.

- National Homeland Security Strategy (July 2002): Directs NCS to help facilitate DHS's efforts to develop comprehensive emergency communications systems.

C.3 Coordinating Agency Authorities

- Federal Communications Commission (FCC): The Communications Act of 1934, as amended by the Telecommunications Act of 1996, is the principal statute governing Federal regulation of the Communications Sector. The act directs the FCC to ensure that radio and wire communications effectively serve the public's interest in the safety of life and property and in the national defense. Additional FCC authorities and policies with network protection equities include the following:

  - E.O. 12472: Directs the FCC to review the policies, plans, and procedures of all entities licensed or regulated by the FCC that are developed to provide NS/EP communications services to ensure that they are consistent with the public interest.

  - Section 0.181, Title 47 of the Code of Federal Regulations: Sets out the duties of the FCC Defense Commissioner, including serving as the principal point of contact for the commission on all NCS-related matters.

  - 47 United States Code (U.S.C.) 308(a): Establishes the FCC's licensing procedures during emergencies.

  - FCC 2nd Report and Order, WT Docket 96-86: Establishes rules and requirements for the NCS Priority Access Service program.

  - FCC Report and Order 88-341: Establishes the regulatory, administrative, and operational framework for the TSP program, which involves the priority restoration and provisioning of any qualified NS/EP communications service. The Office of the Manager NCS administers the TSP program.

  - FCC Report and Order, Notification by Common Carriers of Service Disruptions, CC Docket No. 91-273: Requires wireline carriers to report significant service disruptions to the FCC. Note: Since January 2005, the FCC outage reporting requirement was broadened to cover wireless, cable, and satellite outages.

  - FCC's Communications Security, Reliability, and Interoperability Council (CSRIC): The original CSRIC Charter was filed January 6, 1992. Subsequent charters address specific areas of communications beyond reliability and resilience issues to include interoperability, security, cyber, and emergency services. The charter was also expanded to adapt to the changing scope of the sector, including wireless and public data networks.

- The DOC National Telecommunications and Information Administration (NTIA): The Communications Act of 1934 specifies that all Federal agencies will have their spectrum needs administered and authorized by a separate agency, currently the NTIA. As tasked under E.O.s 12046, 12472, and 12656, the NTIA also serves as the telecommunications policy adviser to the President and as a member of the Joint Telecommunications Resources Board.

- The Defense Production Act: Authorizes the President to require the priority performance of contracts and orders necessary to promote national defense, including critical infrastructure protection and restoration. It also authorizes the President to allocate materials and facilities, as necessary, to promote national defense. Pursuant to the Defense Production Act, regulations promulgated by the DOC in the Defense Priorities and Allocations System (DPAS) permit the assignment of "priority ratings" to certain equipment associated with NS/EP communications services warranting priority treatment if they support authorized programs under Schedule I of the DPAS.

C.4 Other Guidance

- Presidential War Emergency Powers for Telecommunications: Section 706 of the Communications Act of 1934 (47 U.S.C. 606) authorizes the President to exercise certain emergency communications functions during a wartime emergency.

- State and Local Authorities: State and local officials have some jurisdiction over the communications providers within their State or local boundaries, for example:

  - In Maine, the PUC has promulgated rules requiring communications carriers to file maps indicating key utility infrastructure with the commission (Utility Service Area and Infrastructure Maps (chapter 140), Docket No. 2001-284).

  - In Texas, there are State councils and operations centers that coordinate efforts to restore communications after a natural or manmade disaster. Groups within the Texas Office of Homeland Security coordinate the efforts of the State of Texas and private industry in the protection of CIKR. During major emergencies, such as Hurricane Rita and the crash of the space shuttle Columbia, the State Operations Center activates its Emergency Management Council to coordinate efforts within the State agencies and with local jurisdictions and critical infrastructure.

Appendix D: Sector Profile

D.1 Wireline Infrastructure

The wireline component primarily consists of the PSTN, as well as enterprise networks. The PSTN is a domestic communications network accessed by telephones, key telephone systems, PBX trunks, and data arrangements. Completion of the circuit between the call originator and the call receiver requires network signaling in the form of dial pulses or multi-frequency tones. These components are connected by nearly 2 billion miles of fiber and copper cable (physical), have IT systems that monitor and move the data (cyber), and have dedicated staff to ensure service (people). Despite the industry's transition to packet-based networks, the traditional PSTN remains the backbone of the communications infrastructure.

The wireline component has traditionally been divided between IXCs and LECs. Local access and transport areas (LATAs) provide definition to the areas of provisioning responsibilities. Generally, the incumbent LEC companies provided local and intra-LATA toll services, with the IXCs providing interexchange toll services. However, regulatory developments have blurred the lines between those providers. Now, many traditional LECs are evolving to provide long-distance services, and more IXCs are becoming full service providers. In addition, following passage of the Telecommunications Act of 1996, new CLECs entered the local, long-distance, and data services markets, as did some traditional CATV providers. Through their wireline networks, IXCs, LECs, and CLECs are also leading providers of Internet access and broadband services. Future providers may involve non-traditional platforms and infrastructure, such as broadband over power lines.

Key wireline network and transmission elements include the following, many of which are detailed in figure D-1:

- Local Exchange Switching: The traditional local exchange network is a hierarchical structure with end-to-end connections using customer, local, and long-distance networks. This, coupled with an ability to concentrate more traffic over fewer links, has lowered the cost of long-distance traffic to the consumer. However, these same capabilities have resulted in more significant impacts when long-distance links and node and link failures occur.

- Interexchange Switching: The traditional interexchange networks are independent mesh structures that incorporate direct point-to-point connections between nodes.

- Transmission Links: The physical unit of a subnetwork that provides the transmission connection between adjacent nodes.

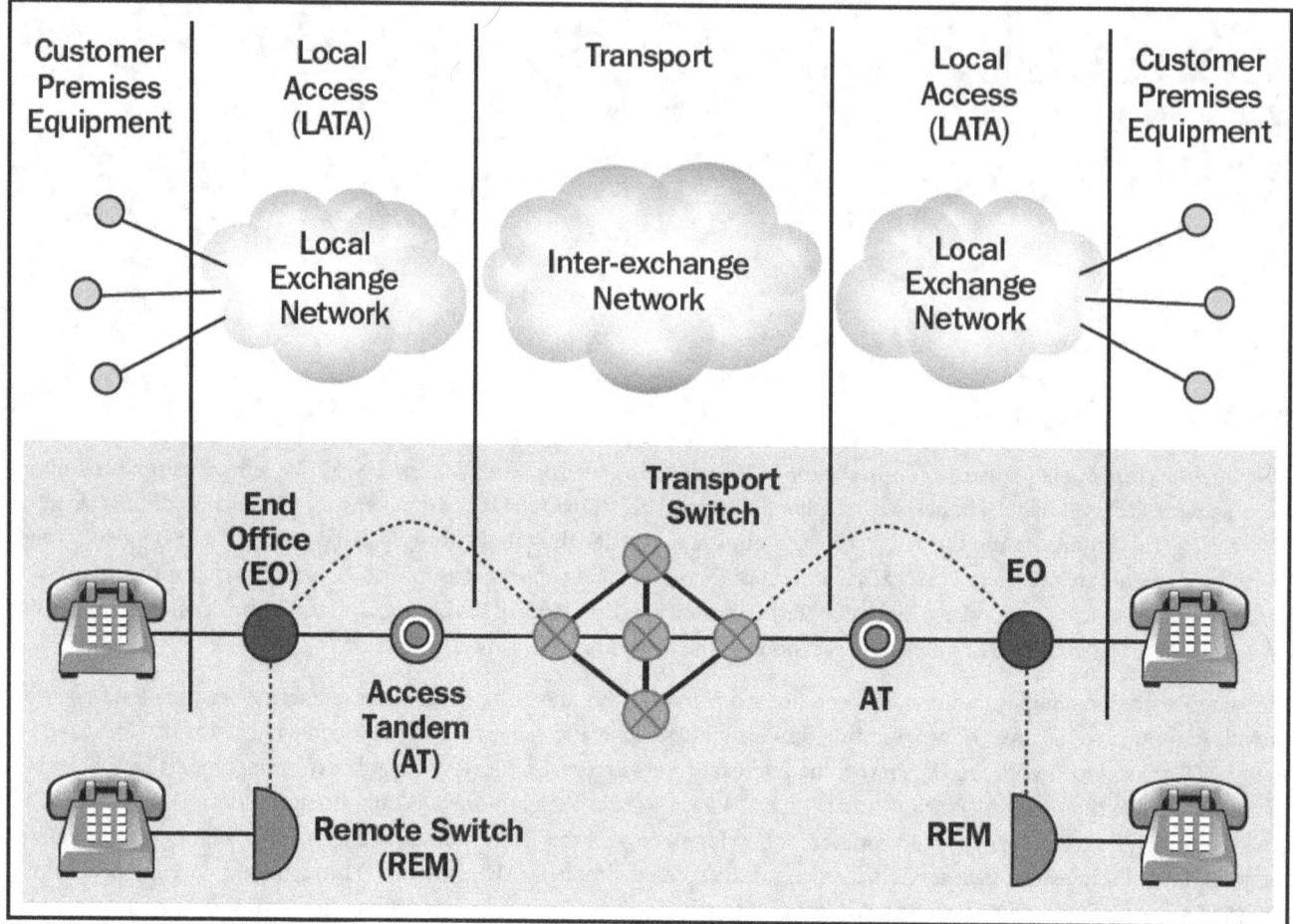

Signaling System Number 7 (SS7). SS7 is a communications protocol that provides signaling and control for various network services and capabilities. SS7 networks are medium-speed (56 or 64 kilobits per second), packet-switched networks that overlay the carriers' circuit-switched networks and provide network control functionality to the PSTN. SS7 is composed of a series of interconnected network elements (e.g., switches, databases, and routing nodes). The SS7 protocol also has significant cyber implications because it affords the interface from circuit-switched (traditional) networks to IP-based networks. Figure D-2 illustrates how the SS7 connects to the wireline network.

Figure D-2: SS7 and Wireline Network Architecture

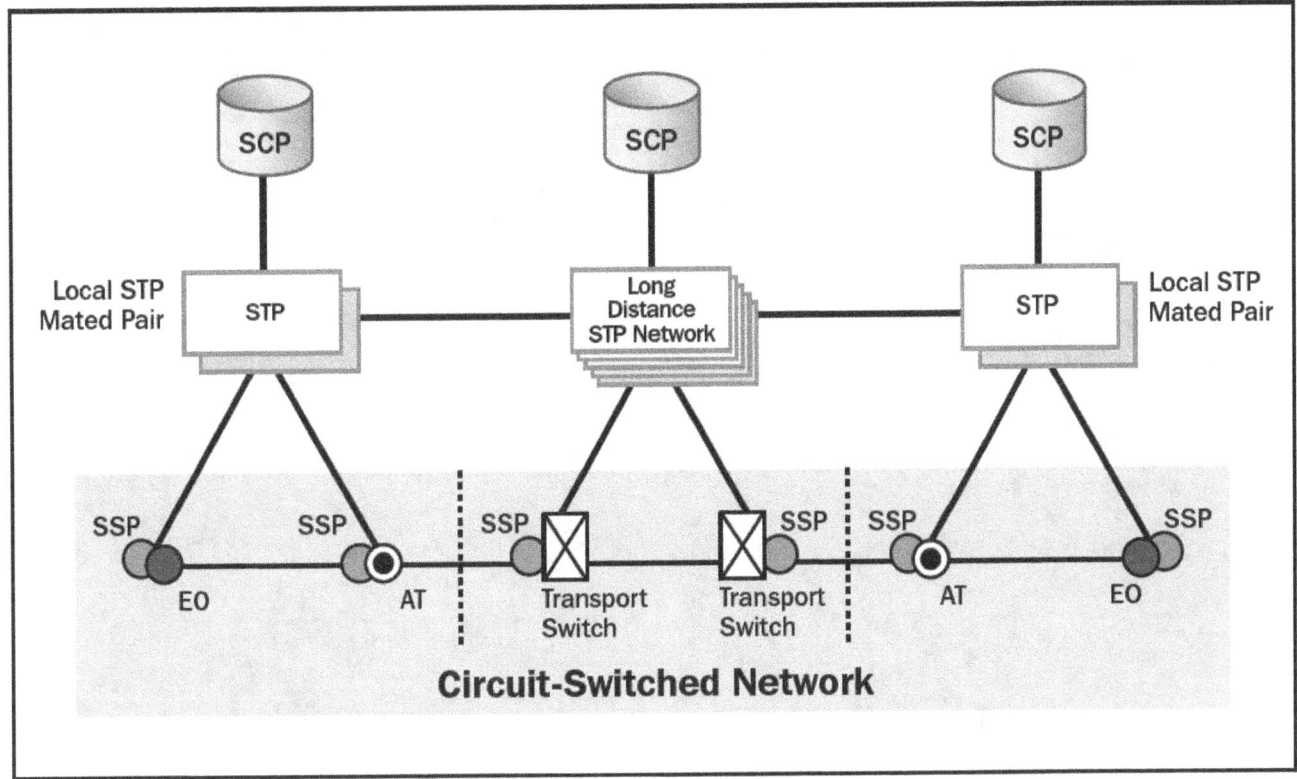

Next-Generation Networks (NGNs). The concept of NGNs considers new realities within the communications industry and can be defined as high-speed, converged circuit-switched and packet-switched networks capable of transporting and routing a multitude of services, including voice, data, video, and multimedia, across variant platforms. NGNs leverage open architecture over a common transport network with an emphasis on optical networking and intelligent or NGN "aware" elements. NGNs seamlessly blend the PSTN and the packet-switched data network and are also called converged networks because they integrate voice and data communications across traditionally divergent fixed and mobile platforms to an increasing array of end-user devices.

Key NGN functional elements (see figure D-3) include the media gateway (MG), the signaling gateway (SG), and the media gateway controller (MGC).

Figure D-3: Next-Generation Networks

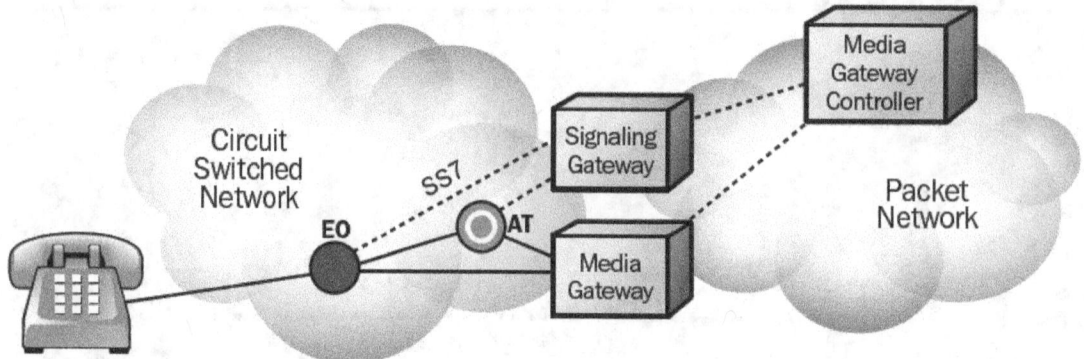

Voice over Internet Protocol (VoIP). VoIP uses the Internet or any other IP-based network to route calls rather than the PSTN with a packet-switched network being used rather than dedicated, circuit-switched telephony transmission lines. Figure D-4 depicts the elements of a VoIP network configuration.

Figure D-4: VoIP Networks

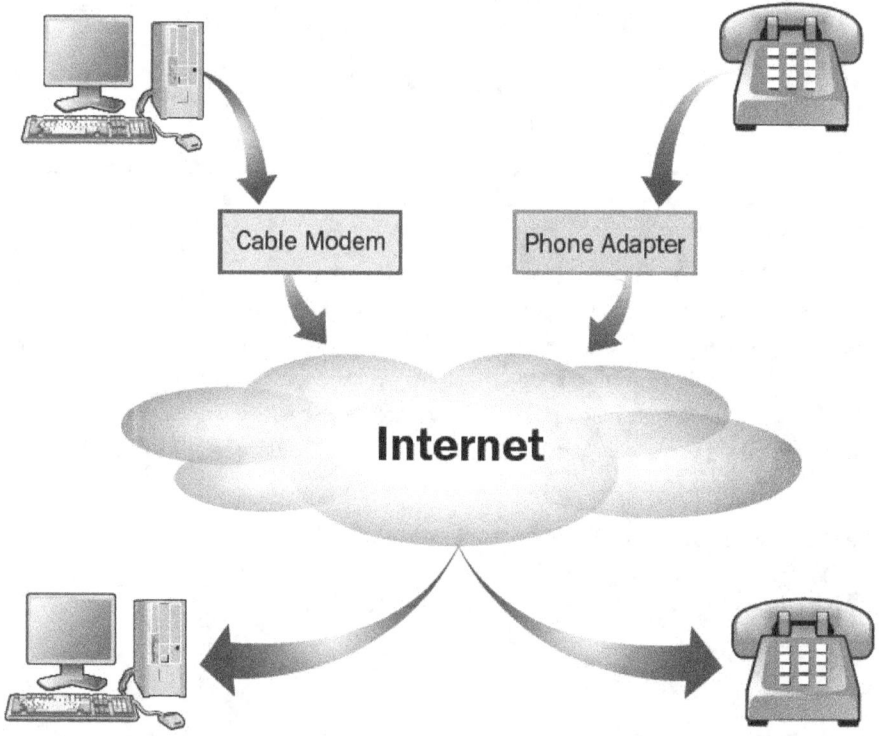

Submarine Cable Networks. Submarine cable networks are long-haul wireline networks constructed across major bodies of water to interconnect networks. Key submarine cable components (see figure D 5) include landing locations/cable heads and switching centers.

Figure D-5: Submarine Cable Architecture

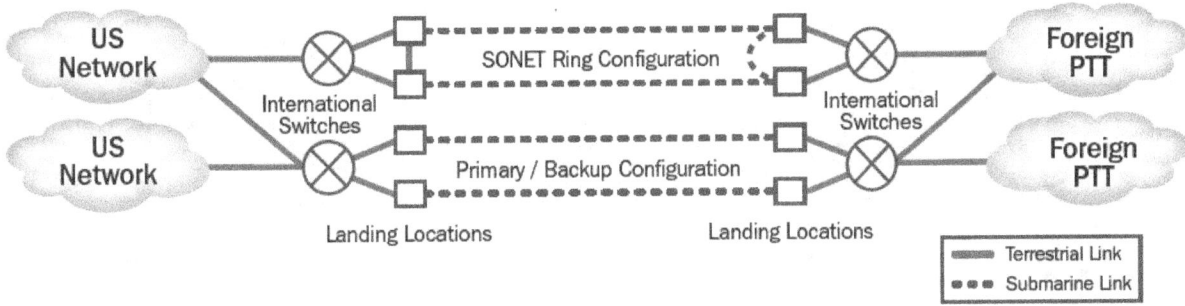

The Internet. The Internet encompasses the global infrastructure of packet-based networks and databases that use a common set of protocols for communicating (see figure D-6). The networks are connected by various transports. The most common examples of Internet access include ordinary telephone lines (dialup); broadband services such as Digital Subscriber Lines (DSL) and cable modems; Integrated Services Digital Network (ISDN); T1 and T3 lines; and interconnected wireless services, infrastructure, and devices.

Figure D-6: Internet Architecture[15]

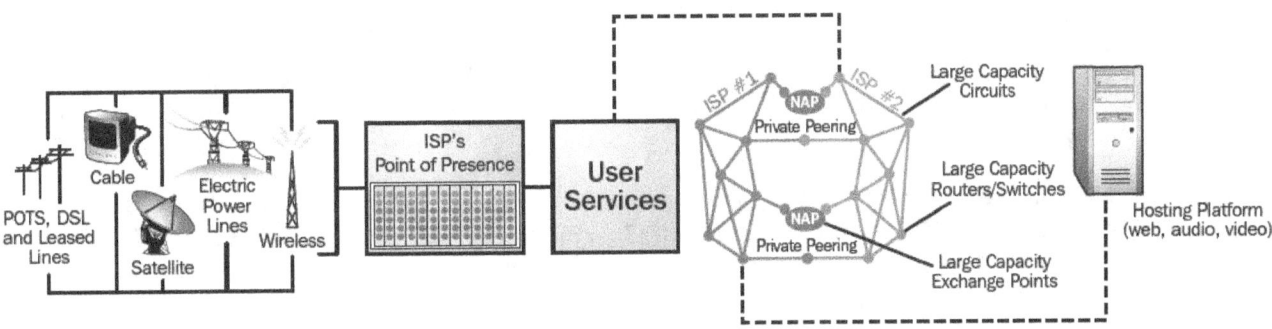

D.2 Wireless Infrastructure

Wireless communications include cellular phone, paging, personal communications services, high-frequency radio, unlicensed wireless, and other commercial and private radio services. Mobile wireless services have become indispensable for businesses and consumers, as well as for public safety needs. According to industry estimates, U.S. mobile market penetration exceeded two-thirds in 2005, with greater levels in the largest metropolitan markets.[16]

A cellular-type Wireless Communications System is an automated, high-capacity system of one or more multichannel base stations designed to provide radio communications services to users over a wide area in a spectrally efficient manner. A cellular-type architectural system operates by dividing a large geographical service area into cells and assigning the same channels to multiple, nonadjacent cells. This design allows channels to be reused, increasing spectrum efficiency. As a subscriber travels across the service area, the call is transferred (handed off) from one cell to another without noticeable interruption. Cellular-type wireless networks are composed of several elements (see figure D-7), including cell sites, mobile switching centers (MSC) and base switching controllers (BSC).

---

[15] Adapted from http://navigators.com/internet_architecture.html.

[16] Forbes.com, August 19, 2005.

Figure D-7: Wireless Network Architecture

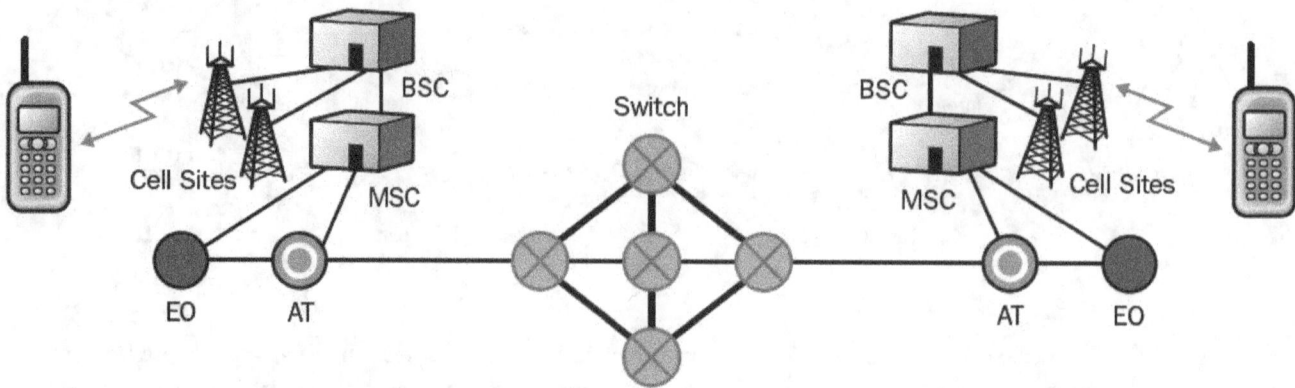

High-frequency (HF) radio (commonly known as shortwave radio) can be used for communication over great distances and between points separated by geographic barriers (e.g., mountains). An HF radio system consists of three basic components: (1) the transmitter/receiver unit (commonly called the transceiver), (2) the antenna, and (3) the power source.

D.3 Satellite Infrastructure

Satellite communications systems deliver data, voice, and video services. Networks may be private and independent of the terrestrial infrastructure or may share common facilities (e.g., a Teleport) and be combined with terrestrial services to deliver information to the intended recipient(s).

Geostationary Earth Orbit (GEO) systems typically require a single satellite for a continental United States (CONUS) footprint and three satellites to have a global footprint. Non-geostationary Low Earth Orbit (LEO) and Middle Earth Orbit (MEO) require numerous satellites for global coverage. A group of satellites working in concert is thus known as a satellite constellation (see figure D-8).

Satellite services exist in several forms:

- Fixed;

- Transportable;

- On the move;

- Handheld (Mobile Satellite Services (MSS)); and

- Broadcast Satellite Services (BSS (public broadcast)).

The technology can deliver two-way point-to-point or mesh converged communications (voice, data, and video) for access and/or backbone services, as well as multicast (video and/or data for distribution of content to large geographically dispersed audiences. MSS services are primarily voice with limited to mid-range data capabilities.

Important satellite network components include ground stations; telemetry, tracking, and command links (TT&Cs); very small aperture terminals (VSATs); and data links (see figure D-8).

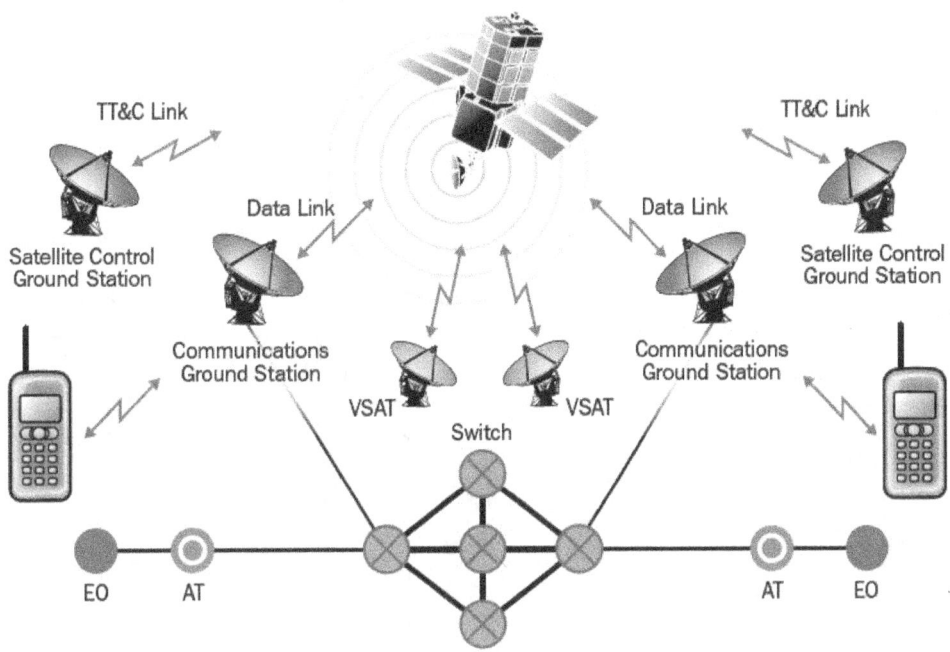

D.4 Cable Infrastructure

The U.S. CATV industry serves approximately 63.1 million basic cable customers, representing a market penetration of 50.3 percent of U.S. television households. The cable industry is composed of approximately 7,791 cable systems. Many of the systems are owned by Multiple-System Operators (MSOs), with 10 major MSOs providing services to about 58 million households. Cable services include analog and digital video programming services, digital telephone service, and high-speed Internet access service.

Most cable systems use a mixture of fiber and coaxial cable that provide bidirectional signal paths to the customer. This HFC architecture effectively segments the cable system into a number of parallel distribution networks. The HFC architecture is beneficial to the cable operator because it improves signal performance and reliability, increases available bandwidth, and is generally easier to maintain than older architecture. The HFC architecture is typically based on a three-level topology, which includes a headend, one or more distribution hubs, and multiple fiber nodes (See figure D-9).

Figure D-9: Cable Network Architecture

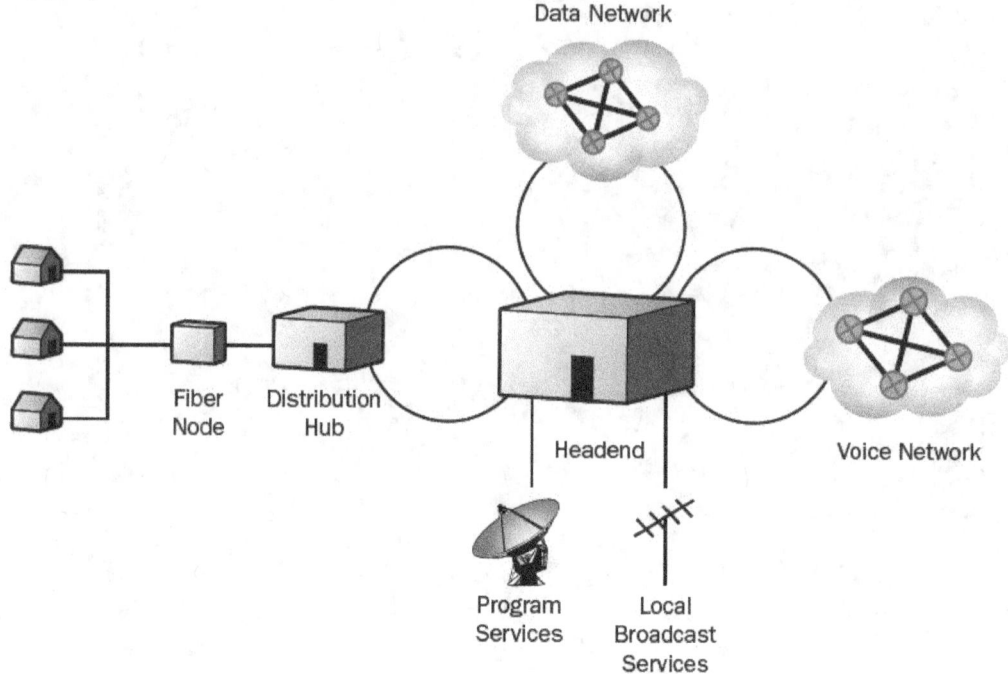

D.5 Broadcasting Infrastructure

There are more than 14,000 radio and 1,700 television broadcasting facilities in the United States. As a group, broadcasting services represent the most pervasive and redundant means of communications to the public and are the only services available at no cost to the consumer. Radio and television broadcasting facilities typically have three principal components: (1) the studio, (2) the transmitter, and (3) the studio-to-transmitter link (STL). Broadcasters typically design multiple levels of redundancy into each of these components, including:

* Main and backup studio facilities;

* Multiple, independent STLs utilizing wireline, wireless, and satellite radio channels; and

* Primary and auxiliary transmitters, towers, and antennas.

Provisions are typically made for backup electrical power using battery backup and diesel/gasoline-powered generators.

Figure D-10: Broadcasting System—Simplified Block Diagram

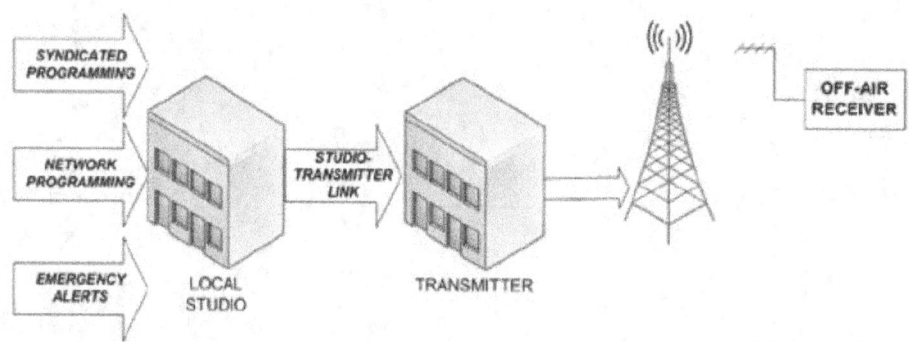

Appendix E: Existing Protective Programs

Protective programs are grouped into two categories: protective actions and preparedness actions. Protective actions involve the methods for selecting the best actions within the time constraints of a fast-moving emergency. Protective measures include measures that describe preparations taken before an emergency situation to ensure that implementation is possible during an emergency. In addition, protective measures include decisionmaking and implementation issues to rapidly reduce the effects of an emergency situation or contamination. Preparedness actions involve activities and measures designed or undertaken to prepare for or minimize the effects of a natural or manmade hazard on the civilian population; to deal with the immediate emergency conditions that would be created by the hazard; and to effectuate emergency repairs to, or the emergency restoration of, vital utilities and facilities destroyed or damaged by the hazard. Preparedness actions also involve the continuous operationally focused process for establishing guidelines, protocols, and standards for planning, training and exercises, personnel qualification and certification, equipment certification, and publication management.

Partnerships such as the NCC, the President's NSTAC, and NSIEs are the basis for many protective programs as a result of their role in information sharing, protective program development, and response and recovery efforts. Communications Sector members are focused on meeting the needs of its sector and customers through protective and preparedness actions and operational plans and procedures to assist in the following:

- Preventing or delaying an incident;

- Determining the potential impact of an incident and detecting it when one occurs;

- Responding to and mitigating the impact of an incident in a manner that enables the sector asset to resume operations quickly; and

- Recovering from an incident.

E.1 Protective Actions

Protective actions include actions that contribute to the deterrence, devaluation, detection, or defense against attacks. At the owner or operator level, protective actions are implemented based on their business continuity requirements. Examples for each of the four categories of protective actions performed by owners and operators are as follows:

- Deter: Facility surveillance and facility and network access controls;

- Devalue: Backup network operations centers and SONET ring networks;

- Detect: Facility alarm systems and network monitoring; and

- Defend: Buffer zones for critical facilities and firewalls on control system networks.

As an organized sector, partnerships serve as the mechanism for enhancing the protection provided by these protective activities. These partnerships foster the sharing of specific information on threats and vulnerabilities, which is crucial to understanding the risks to the sector. Industry shares important information that helps the government to understand the nature of the vulnerabilities and the potential impact if exploited and to report network anomalies. The following are examples of how these partnerships promote awareness and enhance protection:

- As part of its ISAC function, the NCC collects and shares information about threats, vulnerabilities, intrusions, and anomalies.

- NSTAC task forces regularly study the vulnerabilities of the Communications Sector, often recommending new programs and mitigation techniques.

- CSRIC provides recommendations in the form of best practices that provide companies with guidance aimed at improving the overall reliability, interoperability, and security of wireless, wireline, satellite, cable, and public data networks.

- In addition to sharing information on threats with the public network, NSIEs periodically conduct a risk assessment of the public network.

In addition to improving overall sector risk awareness, the NCC plays a critical role in identifying anomalies in the communications network and issuing alerts and warnings through its 24/7 watch center. NCS has developed programs that help provide government officials and communications owners with early warnings of potential threats and attacks on critical physical and cyber infrastructure. The NCC also coordinates and shares information with the NOC, the NICC, and other industry operations centers.

NCS has undertaken protective activities to enhance the Federal Government's communications infrastructure protection efforts. NCS is conducting a study that evaluates the Federal agencies' need for route diversity. The scope of the project includes identification of vulnerabilities of generic government facility communications network architectures, investigating technical mitigation solutions, and developing a Route Diversity Methodology (RDM). The RDM includes an assessment methodology to determine the risk to an agency's communications systems and to apply route diversity mitigation solutions to reduce risk. The employment of route diversity solutions is a preventive strategy for Federal agencies to ensure the availability of communications during crises.

Overall, few Federal-level protective activities exist because the responsibility for protecting the critical infrastructure lies primarily with the private sector. Per the goals outlined in chapter 1, the private sector recognizes its responsibility for protecting its personnel and networks from attack. Operators and carriers voluntarily implement best practices (see appendix G) for developing and implementing protective programs.

E.2 Preparedness Actions

Preparedness actions include actions that mitigate the consequences of an event. The Communications Sector is heavily focused on preparedness actions as a result of the exposure of the networks to natural disasters, as well as intentional or unintentional attacks and actions. The Communications Sector has a solid record for its response and recovery efforts after incidents. Preparedness is coordinated at the company level, inter-company, and between industry and government. Examples of preparedness activities undertaken by industry include the following:

- Respond: Emergency response plans, procedures, and exercises;

- Mitigate: Self-healing networks and redundant signaling systems; and

- Recover: Business continuity plans and mutual-aid agreements.

In most cases, State and local agencies have been designated the leads for preparedness and response. Guiding authorities such as the NRF note that the Federal role is to support the activities of these agencies. At the national level, preparedness activities for the Communications Sector are primarily coordinated through the NCC. In the NCC, industry and government jointly plan and work to support a more endurable national communications system. These planning activities include the development and maintenance of the Operations Plan and supporting SOPs. The SOP provides for Federal communications support to State, local, and tribal government response elements, upon request.

In addition to planning, successful coordination requires training and exercises. The NCS Emergency Response Training (ERT) program ensures readiness, enhances partnerships between industry and government, coordinates communications operational planning among NCS elements, develops emergency response requirements, and provides skilled civilians and reservists during crises and emergencies. NCS regularly conducts Telecommunications ERT seminars for emergency responders and planners that provide support during disasters and emergencies. The seminars provide an overview of current and future communication services and capabilities for use during disasters and emergencies, and aim to improve the SOP (Communications) response and recovery structure. These training curricula address all hazards. NCS also sponsors an annual Regional Managers Conference, for government only, to provide updated information on the evolving roles and responsibilities related to disaster planning and response operations.

NCS conducts internal and external exercises for maintaining expert knowledge of and proficiency in the management, integration, and use of NS/EP communications resources. This effort includes accessing and evaluating NCS operational capabilities through the use of the Emergency Operations Team (EOT). The NCC also conducts several internal exercises annually. These exercises, typically one day long, are designed to test the NCC Watch Center, NCS staff, and EOT members and their operational procedures in response to the entire spectrum of emergencies and disasters. These exercises ensure that NCS has a trained cadre of emergency response personnel and enable the NCC to test its SOPs and operational readiness.

During an event, the NCC coordinates the initiation and reconstitution of NS/EP communications services and facilities. As the operational focus of NCS, the NCC carries out its SOP (Communications) responsibilities under the National Response Framework. The NCC Initial Response Team is the first NCS organization to respond to a crisis, making an initial assessment and alerting the NCC EOT staff, as necessary.

The key partners and users of NCS priority services and programs are responsible for minimizing loss of life and restoring order following a major disaster. These groups include those providing or supporting national security leadership, emergency warning and response, maintenance of public health and safety, maintenance of law and order, and maintenance of economic security. These groups include not only national, State, and local government leaders, but also the senior leadership of the Nation's critical infrastructure and key communications and IT industries and organizations. In addition, the NCS Manager maintains an inventory of industry NGN capabilities that contribute to the reconstitution of NS/EP communications under the SOP of the NRF. The continued success of the programs, listed below, is essential to ensuring the reliability and interoperability of the Federal Government's owned or commercially provided NS/EP communications resources.

- **Government Emergency Telecommunications Service (GETS):** Provides emergency access and priority processing in the local and long-distance segments of the PSTN. This service increases the likelihood that NS/EP personnel can complete critical calls during periods of PSTN disruption and congestion resulting from natural or manmade disasters. GETS supports Federal, State, and local government, industry, and nonprofit organization personnel in performing their NS/EP missions. GETS uses three major types of networks: (1) major long-distance networks, (2) local networks, and (3) government-leased networks.

- **Wireless Priority Service (WPS):** Provides priority Commercial Mobile Radio Service (CMRS) during and after emergencies for NS/EP personnel by ensuring that WPS calls receive the next available radio channel during times of wireless congestion. WPS helps to ensure that key NS/EP personnel can complete critical calls by providing priority access during times of wireless network congestion to key leaders and supporting first responders. In conjunction with GETS, WPS provides an end-to-end solution.

- **Special Routing Arrangement Service (SRAS):** Supports COOP by providing survivable communications linkages to Federal and defense end users over the public network.

- **Next-Generation Priority Service (NGPS):** Develops technology to provide priority service capabilities over IP networks standardize the technology across industry through the commercial standards process, and migrate current priority service features to the technology.

In addition to the priority services programs that aid recovery efforts, NCS administers the TSP program. This program provides the regulatory, administrative, and operational framework for priority restoration and provisioning of NS/EP communication circuits in the event of an emergency. Eligibility for the TSP program extends to Federal, State, and local governments, private industry, or foreign governments that have communications services that support an NS/EP mission.

NCS also administers the Shared Resources (SHARES) HF Radio Program, which enhances information sharing during an event. The SHARES program brings together the existing HF radio resources of Federal, State, and industry organizations when normal communications are destroyed or unavailable. The SHARES program also provides the Federal community with a forum for addressing issues that affect HF radio interoperability.

NCS is also working with OSTP and the NCS COP to develop an NS/EP continuity communications architecture that will reflect emerging threats and potential vulnerabilities arising from network convergence. The objectives of the initiative are to develop an enterprise architecture that is (1) secure, reliable, survivable, and enduring; (2) flexible, mobile, and interoperable; (3) consistent with converged network services and open standards; and (4) supported by the transformation of legacy circuit-switched infrastructure to a service-oriented architecture.

E.3 Internet Security Programs

Various government programs, such as those listed below, improve Internet security to prepare, mitigate, and respond to cyber attacks.

- **United States Computer Emergency Readiness Team (US-CERT):** Leads and coordinates efforts to improve the Nation's cybersecurity posture, promote cyber information sharing, and manage cyber risks to the Nation. US-CERT collaborates with Federal agencies, the private sector, the research community, State and local governments, and international entities. By analyzing incidents reported by these entities and coordinating with national security incident response centers that are responding to incidents on classified and unclassified systems, US-CERT disseminates actionable cybersecurity information to the public.

- **National Cyber Response Coordination Group (NCRCG):** Facilitates the Federal Government's efforts to prepare for, respond to, and recover from physical attacks and cyber incidents that have significant cyber consequences. As a member agency, NCS brings subject matter expertise, established relationships with private industry, and other capabilities in support of the NCRCG's efforts.

- **NET Guard:** Brings together the public sector with the State and local community following an incident that affects information systems and communications networks. The intent of this initiative is to create teams of volunteers from the private sector that could provide technical assistance and resources to the affected community. The program also acts as a clearinghouse for matching the needs of the local government and businesses with available resources in a timely manner.

Appendix F: Communications Sector Key Risk Mitigation Activities

As referenced in chapter 6, key RMAs for the sector are highlighted within this appendix. The following RMAs were identified in the Communications SAR.

Development of Government-to-Government Priority Communications Services via the Government Emergency Telecommunications Service (GETS)

Description of Activity

The GETS program is a White House-directed emergency phone service provided by NCS. GETS supports Federal, State, local, and tribal government; industry; and nongovernmental organization personnel in performing their NS/EP missions. GETS provides emergency access and priority processing in the local and long-distance segments of the PSTN. GETS is intended to be used during an emergency or crisis situation when the PSTN is congested and the probability of completing a call over normal or other alternate telecommunications means has significantly decreased. GETS uses local, long-distance, and government-leased networks to accomplish this goal. Outreach activities are conducted through programs, literature, and conferences. As established by Presidential Directives and FCC rulings, the GETS program reduces risk by increasing the probability that key personnel will be able to complete landline calls when the PSTN is degraded.

Progress Indicators

During Hurricane Gustav in September 2008, NS/EP personnel completed 89 percent of all GETS calls. The majority of the incomplete calls during Gustav were due to infrastructure damage, power outages, and the loss of a critical communications switch in the Baton Rouge area that eliminated the path needed for long-distance services critical to GETS. During Hurricane Ike, also in September 2008, GETS customers completed 97.4 percent of their calls, with a total of 7,226 calls made over eight days. During the inauguration of President Obama, NS/EP callers using GETS completed 99 percent of the more than 700 priority service calls attempted during the inaugural weekend in January 2009.

During FY 2008, priority service call completion rates during emergencies were 97 percent, an increase of 3 percent since FY 2007, and a 7 percent increase over the FY 2008 target rate of 90 percent. Furthermore, the completion rate for the first quarter of FY 2009 equaled 99.3 percent, an additional 2.3 percent increase since FY 2008.

The number of GETS users increased 63,608 from March 31, 2008 to March 31, 2009, with 81 percent of Federal continuity coordinators having access to priority telecommunications services in FY 2008. The average cost of maintaining a priority telecommunications service user dropped $3.10 per user in FY 2008 to $13.90 per user.

Telecommunications Service Priority Program

Description of Activity

The FCC issued a Report and Order (FCC 88-341) on November 17, 1988, that established the TSP System and officially adopted TSP System rules as part of the Code of Federal Regulations. FCC 88-341 assigns the responsibility of TSP administration to the EOP, who delegated the responsibility to NCS. The TSP program is the regulatory, administrative, and operational system authorizing and providing for priority treatment of NS/EP telecommunications services. The TSP program is available to all sectors and organizations (Federal, State, local, and private industry entities) that support or have NS/EP missions and rely on communications to prepare for and respond to emergencies and disaster situations. The TSP program provides service vendors with an FCC mandate for prioritizing service requests by identifying those services that are critical to NS/EP. A telecommunications service with a TSP assignment will receive full attention by the service vendor before a non-TSP service.

The TSP program has two components: restoration and provisioning. A restoration priority applies to telecommunications services to ensure restoration before any other services. A provisioning priority is obtained to facilitate priority installation of new telecommunications services in response to an emergency. In addition to daily operations, TSP Program Office personnel are notified of presidentially declared disasters, activation of the NRF, ESF-2 communications, and COOP plan activations, and are on-call 24/7.

Progress Indicators

The TSP System was available to CIKR partners and participants during the 2009 Presidential Inauguration, providing users with prioritization for restoration in the event that carrier facilities were cut or service degraded. The TSP Program Office also assigned restoration and provisioning priorities during the 2008 hurricane season, the tornados and subsequent flooding in the Midwestern United States, at the Democratic and Republican National Conventions, at Federal Reserve Bank sites, at UN General Assembly 63, during the Ukrainian President's visit to the United States in September 2008, and for operations of U.S. Customs and Border Protection. The total number of circuits enrolled in the TSP program is steadily growing.

NS/EP Priority Telecommunications Service Through Wireless Priority Service

Description of Activity

The NS/EP Priority Telecommunications Service (PTS), which includes the aforementioned GETS, is a White House-directed program that provides the NS/EP user community with specially designed telecommunications services during natural or man-made disasters when conventional communications services are ineffective. These telecommunication services are used to coordinate response and recovery efforts and, under severe conditions, to assist with COOP and COG. In addition to GETS, the NS/EP PTS enhances the ability of NS/EP users to complete calls through a degraded PSTN using WPS during a crisis or emergency situation. WPS is a multicarrier, standards-based national capability that allows priority communications when cellular service availability is limited because of the network congestion that occurs during crisis events. WPS is a nationwide wireless telephone service that complements and interoperates with GETS and provides priority NS/EP telecommunications via selected commercial wireless carriers. WPS calls receive the next available radio channel during times of wireless congestion, which helps to ensure that key NS/EP personnel can complete critical calls by providing priority access to key leaders and supporting first responders.

Progress Indicators

The number of WPS users has increased by approximately 67 percent from the FY 2008 target. The WPS program has grown because of constant promotion by NCS Regional Outreach Coordinators, related booth deployments, and speaking engagements. More than 1,200 new subscriptions were activated during Hurricane Ike. As demonstrated during the 2008 hurricane season, the program stands at a high level of readiness. In July 2008, the DHS Under Secretary for the National Protection and Programs Directorate (NPPD), who also serves as the Manager of NCS, signed a Letter of Understanding that allows the implementation of WPS between the United States and Canada through roaming agreements.

Network Security Information Exchanges

Description of Activity

NCS and NSTAC established the Federal Government NSIE and the NSTAC NSIE in 1991 to provide an information exchange mechanism between industry and government regarding electronic intrusion threats to and the vulnerabilities of the PN. NSIEs focus on technical issues that affect the overall security of the PN, such as unauthorized penetration or manipulation of PSTN computers and software, databases, and other infrastructure that supports NS/EP telecommunication services. NSIEs exchange ideas on technologies and techniques for addressing and mitigating the risks to the PN and its supporting infrastructure. NSIE membership from the Federal Government includes representation from defense, intelligence, homeland security, law enforcement, and civilian Federal departments and agencies. All NSTAC member companies are eligible to participate in the NSTAC NSIE, and each member company appoints a representative to participate in the forum. Collectively, NSIEs hold meetings every two months to share information and engage in discussions on threats and incidents that affect the PN's software elements and network vulnerabilities, and to discuss possible remedies, including event correlation and monitoring, security metrics, and NSIE security priorities. Between meetings, NSIEs engage in information sharing through the US-CERT portal.

Progress Indicators

Since June 1991, the Federal Government and NSTAC NSIEs have met jointly 110 times. During 2008 and 2009, NSIEs frequently used the US-CERT secure portal to collaborate on urgent security concerns. NSIE members established a forum in which to address the recent increase in circuit card thefts, identify the root cause of the problem, and determine whether NSIEs could collectively provide solutions. Domestic and international partners from public and private sector organizations worked together to construct a database of stolen card information that vendors could use to identify illicit material in the gray and black markets. The forum continues to engage major vendors and is working to develop a Web interface for the database.

While U.S., U.K., and Canadian NSIEs have engaged in information-sharing activities and annual meetings since 2007, NSIE expanded its international partnership during the June 2008 Multilateral NSIE Meeting in Banff, Alberta, Canada, which included counterparts from Canada, the United Kingdom, Australia, and New Zealand. Based on the value of the partnership, government officials from Australia and New Zealand are considering establishing similar groups in their respective countries.

During the 2008–2009 NSTAC reporting cycle, NSIE members received briefings on digital forensics, PCII, netflow analysis, the Comprehensive National Cybersecurity Initiative, cyber threats, cyber prosecution trends and cases, DoD cyber exercises, and GPS security.

Disaster Information Reporting System to Increase Government Situational Awareness

Description of Activity

In support of NCS, the FCC Public Safety and Homeland Security Bureau launched the Disaster Information Reporting System (DIRS) on September 11, 2007. DIRS is a voluntary, Web-based system used by the Communications Sector to report communications infrastructure status and situational awareness information to sector partners in the FCC and DHS. Access to the DIRS Web site is limited to the FCC and NCC Watch. In the event of a major or catastrophic disaster, NCS requires timely, accurate reporting on the stability of the communications infrastructure. The manager of the NCS disseminates DIRS and requests activation and deactivation of DIRS from the NCC based on influencing factors and triggers. DIRS is used during times of crisis, particularly in a disaster area in support of restoration efforts, and provides a snapshot in time. As communications recovery status changes rapidly, DIRS should not be viewed as real-time status because reporting can be as much as 24 hours old.

During the 2008 hurricane season, DIRS was activated for Tropical Storm Fay and for hurricanes Gustav and Ike. Participating communications segments include wireline, wireless, cable, and broadcast. Draft DIRS SOPs were released within NCS on March 23, 2009, with a final SOP release date of April 15, 2009, in time for the start of the 2009 hurricane season.

Enhanced Government/Communications Sector Information Sharing via the NCC and the Communications Information Sharing and Analysis Center

Description of Activity

Both the NCC and C-ISAC support and facilitate the information-sharing environment to ensure CIKR protection through regular meetings of CIKR partners across government and with private industry. The role of the NCC is to assist in the initiation, coordination, restoration, and reconstitution of NS/EP communications services or facilities under all conditions, crises, or emergencies. The NCC serves as a joint industry-government operations center with an operational mission to coordinate response and restoration of the communications infrastructure during an incident. The NCC has five resident industry members[17] and more than 40 additional members representing 95 percent of wireline and wireless service providers; cable, satellite, and ISPs; equipment vendors; and associations.

Through its ISAC function, NCC partners actively share information regarding threats, vulnerabilities, intrusions, and anomalies. As part of the ISAC mission, information regarding threats, vulnerabilities, intrusions, and anomalies is collected from the communications industry and the government and is then analyzed with the goal of averting or mitigating impacts on communications infrastructure.

Progress Indicators

The NCC's C-ISAC expanded its membership to include satellite and broadcast representatives. The NCC tracked and analyzed approaching storms and conducted daily conference calls with industry and government partners during the 2008 hurricane season to coordinate pre- and post-landfall staging, access, security, and fuel response activities in coordination with ESF-2 support elements and industry liaisons during the following:

- Hurricanes Bertha, Dolly, Gustav, Hanna, Ike, and Kyle, and tropical storms Arthur, Cristobal, Edouard, Fay, Josephine, and Laura;
- California wildfires;
- Middle East cable cuts;
- State of the Union address;
- Iowa and Midwestern floods;
- Democratic and Republican Conventions;
- New York City GPS interference; and
- The Group of 20 Global Economic Summit.

C-ISAC participated in NCC Day activities with DHS, NCS, and NCC senior leadership to discuss the unique industry-government partnership and the role that C-ISAC plays in NS/EP disaster response. Additionally, C-ISAC participated with NCS in the ESF-2 Winter Training Workshop and NLE 02-2008 designed to test the ability of the Federal Government and private industry to respond to incidents of national significance.

---

[17] NCC resident members are AT&T, Qwest, Sprint, Verizon, and Verizon Business.

Communications Standards Development for NS/EP Functions on NGNs

Description of Activity

The Communications Sector is both transforming and augmenting traditional circuit switched networks to incorporate the use of technologies based on IP. Voice, video, and data function on one IP-based network technology, and eventually all services will evolve into IP-based end-to-end services. This universal evolution has created new challenges for ensuring that the government can fulfill its NS/EP priority communications responsibilities for government leaders and decision-support officials. As the communications industry continues to make technological advancements, GETS and WPS functionality may be lost because IP-based data networks do not possess the same functionality of priority or dedicated connections as those currently found on traditional telephone networks.

Progress Indicators

To facilitate NS/EP NGN efforts, NCS supported the 2008 Global MultiService Forum Interoperability demonstration of NS/EP NGN priority service enhancements. The 2008 demonstration is continually leveraged to perform proof-of-concept testing on emerging NS/EP NGN technologies. NCS continues to utilize modeling, prototyping, and standards development to assist with an Internet-protocol Multimedia Subsystem (IMS) industry requirements (IR) process that includes service providers, vendors, and standards bodies. The IMS IR process supports the defining of NS/EP requirements for the NGN, and NCS issued multiple NGN Access NS/EP IMS IR in December 2009.

To ensure NS/EP communications services and functionality on the NGN, the transition is divided into three phases:

- **Phase 1: Implement Priority VoIP Capability**

  - Increment 1: Implement priority VoIP capability in the major core networks (e.g., AT&T, Verizon Business, and Sprint) (*current program emphasis*)

  - Increment 2: Implement priority wireless access VoIP communications capability (*for future investigation*)

  - Increment 3: Implement priority wireline access VoIP communications capability (*for future investigation*)

- **Phase 2: Implement Priority Video Service Capability** (*for future investigation*)

- **Phase 3: Implement Priority Data Service Capability** (*for future investigation*)

In addition, the communications industry continues to improve its infrastructure by investing billions of dollars to further infrastructure development. Broadband providers invested $62.5 billion to build out, maintain, and improve their networks in 2007, compared to $45 billion in 2003. Wireless licensees together invested an average of $24.5 billion per year in their networks from 2001 to 2006.

NCS Directive 3-10

Description of Activity

NSPD-51/HSPD-20 established a comprehensive program designed to ensure the survival of the Nation's constitutional form of government and the continuation of the performance of NEFs under all conditions. The Manager of NCS coordinates publishing of communications capabilities required by this directive, conducts testing and develops a quarterly compliance report on the communications requirements, and annually develops recommended updates to the set of minimum continuity communications requirements for consideration by the NCS COP and DHS.

NCS Directive 3-10, Minimum Requirements for Continuity Communications Capabilities (July 25, 2007), establishes policy, explains the legal and regulatory basis, assigns responsibilities to departments and agencies, establishes a minimum set of communications requirements for departments and agencies, and maintains continuity alternate operating facilities. NCS Directive 3-10 intends to establish a Federal inter-agency communications baseline of minimum requirements that support the execution of primary mission essential functions (PMEFs) in support of NEFs and that enable senior leadership to collaborate, develop policy recommendations, and act under all circumstances. This directive also establishes minimum requirements to facilitate ensured communications among the President, the President's staff, EOP personnel, Cabinet Secretaries, and other senior leadership during a crisis.

Progress Indicators

NCS Directive 3-10 establishes an inter-agency baseline of minimum communications requirements that support Communications Sector CIKR resilience. The associated monthly compliance testing provides a continuous basis for improvement.

Education and Outreach Initiatives to Enhance CIKR Protection

Description of Activity

The Communications Sector engages in CIKR protection outreach support with users of NS/EP communications and critical infrastructure and with CIKR partners at the State, regional, local, tribal, and territorial levels. Initiatives are geared toward reaching out to CIKR partners or representatives who require education on various CIKR protective platforms or services to build a foundation of individual skill sets and national prevention, protection, and recovery capabilities.

NCS performs outreach at the Federal, State, and local levels with key officials and emergency managers through RCCs. These individuals attend emergency management meetings, conferences, and establish POCs for priority services. The RCCs accomplish the following:

- Develop relationships with Federal, State, regional, local, and industry communicators;

- Increase the awareness of State emergency communications managers on the need for access, security, and fuel in response to a crisis;

- Gain pre-disaster knowledge of State communications plans and gaps;

- Participate in communications planning efforts and related exercises;

- Represent NCS at Regional Interagency Steering Committee and Regional Emergency Communications Coordination Working Group meetings; and

- Support State ESF-2 communications entities during an emergency or disaster activation as the DEC Branch Manager, Deputy DEC Branch Manager, or Lead Communications Restoration Team.

Progress Indicators

NCS outreach activity has provided connectivity among NCS, State and local governments, and emergency managers. RCCs provide initial personal contact with security response partners. The efforts of the RCCs have helped industry and government partners overcome issues related to access, credentialing, and fuel during critical response efforts.

NCS is the coordinator for ESF-2 under the NRF for all-hazards response (e.g., hurricanes). ESF-2 supports tactical communications and the restoration of communications infrastructure, including recovery from cyber attacks (in coordination with NCSD), during incidents that require a coordinated Federal response. Outreach activities that help to educate local response partners and ensure communications response were a consideration in local exercises and in disaster response planning documents.

Preparedness activities coordinated by the RCCs allowed the NCC, industry, and local officials to share information and create a common operating picture for communications.

Exercise and Training Initiatives to Enhance CIKR Protection

Description of Activity

To ensure proper response during emergencies, industry and government develop exercises around specific scenarios to test and improve response and recovery capabilities. Exercises and training may involve many components, including analysis, the utilization of models to identify potential impacts on the communications infrastructure, representation of actual impacts on the infrastructure, and tracking of restoration activities to inform key government officials on the overall progress of restoration efforts. Exercises and training ensure steady-state protection measures and plans through participation in the National Exercises Program and NCS Emergency Response Training and Exercise Support. NCS is required to participate in all Tier 1 exercises, where odd-year exercises include major COOP elements and even-year exercises include limited, internal COOP exercises. Tier 1 and Tier 2 exercises appear on the Homeland Security Exercise and Evaluation Program National Exercise Schedule. Tier 1 exercises focus on U.S. government-wide strategy and policy; Tier 2 exercises focus on Federal strategy and policy; Tier 3 exercises include other Federal exercises, including operational, tactical, or organizational; and Tier 4 exercises have a State, local, tribal, territorial, or private sector focus.

Progress Indicators

The Communications Sector participated in exercises that tested and evaluated its analytical capabilities in response to various scenarios. In preparation for the 2008 hurricane season, the ESF-2 exercises assessed the capabilities of Federal, State, and local governments and private industry in responding to catastrophic events. DHS sponsored Eagle Horizon 2008, which was a partnership of NCS, the General Services Administration, the FCC, NTIA, FEMA, and USDA.

The Department held traditional classroom training for the DEC Branch Directors in May 2008, and one resulting recommendation was to develop a training series to prepare the entire team for a disaster. Subsequently, the Department developed a series of ESF-2 teleconference training topics, and the first training took place in July 2008. Teleconference training covered such topic areas as preparation for deployment, organization of the DEC Branch, the Robert T. Stafford Disaster Relief and Emergency Assistance Act, and the capabilities of the PSAP 911 emergency services centers.

During the reporting period, NCS modified the training and exercise program to reinforce the role of ESF-2 personnel and to improve each individual's proficiencies with revised plans, procedures, and operational support systems. Destructive hurricane seasons have cemented the need for traditional ESF-2 conferences to continue to address the emergency response needs of a catastrophic event of the magnitude of Hurricane Katrina. Other exercises conducted, attended, and planned include the following:

- November 2008, ESF-2 Winter Conference, Federal Emergency Communications Coordinator (FECC)/DEC Branch leadership tabletop exercise (TTX);
- December 2008, Inauguration Preparedness Workshop;
- May 2009, FEMA Operations 2009 Hurricane Preparedness TTX;
- May 2009, NCS Hurricane Preparedness Workshop;
- June 2009, Eagle Horizon 2009 Continuity-of-Operations Full-Scale Exercise;
- July 2009, NLE 2009 Terrorism Prevention Exercise;
- September 2009, Washington, D.C., Command and Control Full-Scale Exercise;

- 2009 (ongoing), National Exercise Planning Efforts;

- April 2010, NCS/ESF-2 Operation Seattle Shake;

- May 2010, NLE 2010;

- May 2010, Eagle Horizon 10;

- September 2010, Cyber Storm III;

- May 2011, NLE 2011;

- NLE 2011, Regional Preparation Exercises;

- ESF-2 Exercise Eagle Horizon;

- NLE 02-2008 Analytical Support;

- United States Northern Command Vigilant Shield 2009 Exercise;

- State of California Golden Guardian Exercise Support and Region Characterization;

- State of Texas Rehearsal-of-Concept Drill;

- New Madrid Exercise;

- Presidential Joint Telecommunications Resources Board;

- New Jersey Exit-14 Exercise;

- The DHS Office of Infrastructure Protection's Regional Resilience Assessment Program (RRAP);

- Radiological Dispersion Device Tabletop Exercise;

- FEMA, Washington State, U.S. Army Corp of Engineers, and U.S. Department of Energy 2009 Dam Sector Exercise Series;

- Research Triangle Park RRAP;

- Chicago Financial District RRAP;

- Joint NCS/National Cyber Security Division Cyber Exercise, late 2008/early 2009; and

- FEMA 2009 Hurricane Season Tabletop Exercise.

Training during the reporting period included the following:

- Distance learning training series;

- ESF-2 Winter Training Conference;

- Individual Mobilization Augmentee (IMA) Program;

- NCC 2009 Hurricane Preparedness Workshop with industry and government partners; and

- ESF-2 team member training teleconferences (ongoing initiative).

NCS continued to sponsor the IMA program, which relies on U.S. Army Reserve personnel to augment telecommunications response activities. The IMA program provides a surge capability to assist NCS staff or for deployment to regional locations during disaster response and planning as associated with ESF-2 operations. In response to the increased frequency and duration of duty deployments, the NCS IMA Unit increased its personnel strength to the current roster of 20 officers. Officers from the IMA Unit joined the NCS Regional Managers to represent ESF-2 during the Top Officials 4 Exercise and NLE 02-2008. In August 2008, three IMA officers joined an ESF-2 team that was deployed for on-site support during the Democratic National

Convention. Furthermore, the IMA Unit also provided extensive staffing support for ESF-2 operations during hurricanes Dolly, Gustav, Hanna, and Ike.

Communications Sector-Specific Risk Assessments

Description of Activity

In support of the NIPP risk management framework, the Communications Sector strategically carries out risk assessments to examine topics related to physical and cyber risks specific to the Communications Sector. The NSRA, completed in April 2008, comprehensively evaluated the sector's exposure to risk by analyzing the three factors that the NIPP uses to define risk: threats, vulnerabilities, and consequences. The NSRA Working Group focused on those threats with which DHS is most concerned, specifically, threats described by FEMA in the National Planning Scenarios and by HITRAC in the 2007 SHIRA. The working group concluded that these two sources provided a well-rounded set of threats that addressed the all-hazards approach outlined in the NIPP.

The NSRA identified Communications Sector gaps to be addressed in the future. On the basis of the risk analysis of physical threats, the NSRA Working Group concluded that single incidents present no substantial risk to the national communications infrastructure because of the resilience and redundancy of the core network, signaling, databases, and operations management. However, by comparison, access networks and local and regional communications are more vulnerable to these incidents. Local and regional disruptive effects on communications may have substantial impacts (or national consequences) if such communications support critical users or functions.

Progress Indicators

The Communications Sector is scoping follow-on activities to the 2008 NSRA. The Communications Sector realizes that this activity is critical to the sector because it actively and uniquely identifies risks within the sector. Because the NSRA follow-on activity has yet to begin, other sector assessment activity is ongoing under other protective programs.

Cross-Sector Dependency Analysis

Description of Activity

Cross-sector dependency analyses reflect the results of both qualitative and analytical risk analyses that consider threats, vulnerabilities, and consequences. As such, these assessments determine the magnitude and duration of effects based on reliable threat data using both risk and sector experts. Based on research, sector experts determine the key sectors that the Communications Sector depends on to remain operational. Each analysis demonstrates the Communications Sector's dependence on other sectors; assists other sectors in the assessment of communications dependencies for high-risk infrastructure; and identifies high-risk items from other sectors, such as the Transportation Systems Sector for timely fuel delivery to critical network facilities, for collateral damage considerations to the Communications Sector.

Progress Indicators

The NCS COP established the CDEPWG to address the recommendations of the TEPI report as they pertained to NS/EP communications, as well as a broad range of issues resulting from the Communications Sector's dependence on electric power. CDEPWG engaged in numerous activities to study and evaluate the sector's potential to mitigate and recover from a long-term outage. Many recommendations affected the Communications and Energy Sectors.

In addition to the activities of CDEPWG, NCS performed a series of risk assessments on its ability to perform its MEFs. The risk assessments examined a number of high-consequence threat scenarios, all of which could affect the Energy and the Communications Sectors. In several of these event scenarios, the Energy Sector was unable to produce power for extended

---

periods of time, resulting in the loss of the availability of multiple communications networks. The purpose of these activities was to develop a reliable and repeatable methodology that can be used to evaluate the ability of other departments and agencies to perform their MEFs from a communications perspective under adverse conditions.

Short-Term Analytical Initiatives

Description of Activity

The Communications Sector engages in various short-term analytical efforts to support quick-turnaround information requests. Analysis is characterized by a flexible and repeatable framework with quick-turnaround capabilities. A range of scopes and activities fall into this RMA. Site-specific analysis examines data on telecommunications infrastructure at specific sites or locations of concern and determines the potential impacts on the infrastructure or area. Data from incident and event responses and analysis provide input for pre- and post-incident or event scenarios. Concentration analysis identifies the potential risks to the sector based on infrastructure concentration points in specific locations. They assess how the damage at a concentration point could affect a larger segment of the infrastructure. Activities often include analyses of the telecommunications infrastructure and impacts from various classes of events.

Progress Indicators

During the reporting period, the sector conducted four types of analyses: (1) site-specific analyses, (2) incident and event responses and analyses, (3) a concentration analysis, and (4) short-term analyses. Data from these analyses are being used to reduce risk across the sector. Additionally, these assessments are assisting the development of future assessment activity.

Site-Specific Analyses

Site-specific analyses provide analysis of the telecommunications infrastructure and determine the impacts as they pertain to limited-scope sites. Site-specific analyses conducted during the reporting period included:

- Louisiana cellular infrastructure;
- Democratic and Republican National Conventions analyses;
- Alaska submarine cable telecommunications analysis; and
- 2009 Presidential Inauguration analytical support.

Incident and Event Reponses and Analyses

NCS conducted incident and event responses and analyses in collaboration with the NCC in support of emergency response operations to provide an analysis of the telecommunications infrastructure and determine telecommunications impacts resulting from various classes of events. Incident and event responses and analyses conducted during the reporting period included:

- Southern Illinois earthquake telecommunications assessment;
- California wildfires;
- June 2008 Midwest flooding communications and infrastructure analysis;
- Tropical Storm Fay Pre-Landfall telecommunications analysis;
- Hurricane Dolly telecommunications analysis;
- Pre-Landfall Hurricane Gustav telecommunications analysis and NS/EP support;
- Pre-Landfall Hurricane Hanna telecommunications analysis and NS/EP support;

- Pre-Landfall Hurricane Ike telecommunications analysis and NS/EP support;

- Post-Landfall Hurricane Gustav telecommunications analysis and NS/EP support;

- Post-Landfall Hurricane Ike DIRS telecommunications analysis;

- Post-Landfall Hurricane Ike telecommunications analysis and NS/EP support;

- Hurricane Ike restoration trend analysis;

- Sprint-Cogent peering severance support; and

- Hurricane Season 2008 After-Action Report.

Concentration Analysis

NCS conducted a concentration analysis to identify bridges and tunnels with concentrations of telecommunications fiber crossings and the physical telecommunications infrastructure within metropolitan areas and across the United States. During FY 2008, regional concentration studies continued for major metropolitan regions within the United States, and core network analysis continued to identify the routes where large volumes of telecommunications traffic are supported and the locations where infrastructure is concentrated.

Short-Term Analyses

Short-term analyses addressed the telecommunications infrastructure and impacts with respect to various natural disasters and power outages that occurred during the reporting period, as well as national special events such as national conventions. During this reporting period, short-term analyses were conducted on the California wildfires, the Democratic and Republican National Conventions, the Miami power outage, the June 2008 Midwestern floods, Hurricane Dolly, and a site-specific request from the NPPD Under Secretary.

Regional Characterizations

NCS conducted regional characterizations to provide an assessment of nationwide critical telecommunications assets and networks to assess and identify high-risk areas prior to an emergency and during emergency response operations. Each characterization provides an analysis of a significant regional communications agency and site, and the results of each characterization are incorporated into NCS analytical tools and models to support other assessments. The following regional characterizations were conducted during the reporting period:

- New regional characterizations: Los Angeles; New York City; the National Capital Region; the New Madrid Seismic Zone; and Norfolk, Virginia.

- Updates to previously conducted characterizations to include new data and design elements, and incorporation of high-risk areas: San Francisco, Miami, Philadelphia, Boston, Chicago, Dallas, Seattle, and Atlanta.

- New Preparedness Regional Characterizations of telecommunications infrastructure throughout the United States and of the interaction with other infrastructure and sectors examined: Alabama-Mississippi-Louisiana Coast; Boise, Iowa; Florida Mainland; Florida Panhandle; Hawaii; Houston; Jacksonville, Mississippi; New Madrid Seismic Zone; New Orleans; Norfolk, Virginia; St. Louis, Missouri; and Tampa, Florida.

- Updates to previously completed Preparedness Regional Characterizations in the metropolitan areas of Atlanta, Boston, Chicago, Dallas-Fort Worth, Los Angeles, Miami, New York City, the National Capital Region, Philadelphia, San Francisco, and Seattle.

Appendix G: Communications Sector Best Practices

The Communications Sector supports the use of best practices to aid in the implementation of CIKR protective measures. The NIPP encourages private sector owners and operators to adopt and implement those practices that are appropriate and applicable at the specific sector enterprise, individual facility, and system levels.

Best practices are derived from insights from the historic technical support experience of individual companies to address communications infrastructure vulnerabilities. Best practices are presented to the industry only after sufficient diligence and deliberation over conceptual issues and particular wording of the practice. The goals developed throughout the CSSP consider the many dimensions of the protective spectrum. In many cases, sector partners leverage existing programs and best practices to set the sector goals for securing physical, cyber/logical, and human elements. Industry partners support best practices processes, although because of the sector's diversity, true sector-wide risk management and sector-specific best practices are difficult to define.

The FCC has two industry advisory committees that develop best practices. CSRIC provides recommendations in the form of voluntary best practices that provide companies with guidance aimed at improving the overall reliability, interoperability, and security of networks. CSRIC best practices result from broad industry cooperation that engages considerable voluntary resources. Table G-1 lists CSRIC best practices categories.

MSRC has similar processes for developing voluntary best practices for the broadcasting industry. MSRC is an FCC Federal advisory committee focused on ensuring the optimal reliability, robustness, and security of the broadcast and multichannel video programming distribution (MVPD) industries in emergency situations. MSRC best practices focus on physical security, backup power, redundant communications, and redundant facilities. MSRC best practices can be found at **www.mediasecurity.org**.

Use of CSRIC and MSRC best practices remains voluntary; they are not mandated by government. Not every recommendation will be appropriate for every company and circumstance.

Table G-1: CSRIC Best Practices Categories

Access Control	Facilities-Transport	Physical Security
Buildings	Fire	Fire
Business Continuity	Guard Force	Guard Force
Contractors and Vendors	Hardware	Hardware
Corporate Ethics	Human Resources	Human Resources
Cybersecurity	Network Design	Network Design
Disaster Recovery	Network Elements	Network Elements
Documentation	Network Interoperability	Network Interoperability
Emergency Preparedness	Network Operations	Network Operations
Essential Services	Network Provisioning	Network Provisioning